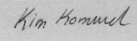

Kim Kommel

P9-CEK-252

SUNDIATA

SUNDIATA

an epic of old Mali

D. T. Niane

Translated by G. D. Pickett

Longman

Longman Group UK Limited,
Longman House, Burnt Mill, Harlow,
Essex CM20 2JE, England
and Associated Companies throughout the world.

First published as Longman African Classic 1986
Eleventh impression 1990

Produced by Longman Group (FE) Ltd
Printed in Hong Kong

ISBN 0-582-64259-0

Contents

Preface   vii

The Words of the Griot Mamadou Kouyaté   1

The First Kings of Mali   2

The Buffalo Woman   4

The Lion Child   12

Childhood   15

The Lion's Awakening   18

Exile   26

Soumaoro Kanté: The Sorcerer King   38

History   40

The Baobab Leaves   43

The Return   47

The Names of the Heroes   54

Nana Triban and Balla Fasséké   56

Krina   59

The Empire   70

Kouroukan Fougan *or* The Division
   of the World   73

Niani   79

Eternal Mali   83

Notes   85

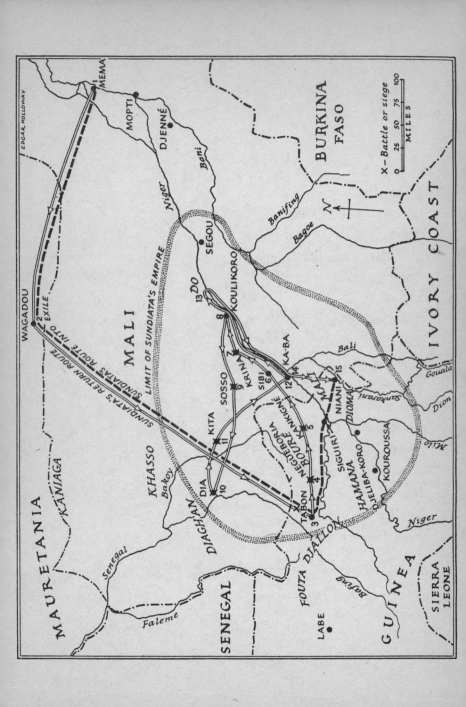

Preface

This book is primarily the work of an obscure griot from the village of Djeliba Koro in the circumscription of Siguiri in Guinea. I owe everything to him. My acquaintance with Mandingo country has allowed me greatly to appreciate the knowledge and talent of Mandingo griots in matters of history.

However, from now on an ambiguity must be cleared up. Nowadays when we speak of 'griots' we think of that class of professional musicians fashioned to live on the backs of others. When we say 'griot' we think of those numerous guitarists who people our towns and go to sell their 'music' in the recording studios of Dakar or Abidjan.

If today the griot is reduced to turning his musical art to account or even to working with his hands in order to live, it was not always so in ancient Africa. Formerly 'griots' were the counsellors of kings, they conserved the constitutions of kingdoms by memory work alone; each princely family had its griot appointed to preserve tradition; it was from among the griots that kings used to choose the tutors for young princes. In the very hierarchical society of Africa before colonization, where everyone found his place, the griot appears as one of the most important of this society, because it is he who, for want of archives, records the customs, traditions and governmental principles of kings. The social upheavals due to the conquest oblige the griots to live otherwise today; thus they turn to account what had been, until then, their fief, viz. the art of eloquence and music.

Nonetheless, one can still find the griot almost in his ancient setting, far from the town, in the old villages of Mali like Ka-ba (Kangaba), Djeliba Koro, Krina, etc., which can boast of still preserving the customs of the times of their ancestors. Generally, in every village of old Mali there is a griot family which conserves historical tradition and teaches it; more usually we find one

vii

village of traditionists to each province, thus: Fadama for Hamana province (Kouroussa, Guinea); Djééla (Droma, Siguiri); Keyla (Republic of Mali), etc.

Unfortunately the West has taught us to scorn oral sources in matters of history, all that is not written in black and white being considered without foundation. Thus, even among African intellectuals, there are those who are sufficiently narrow-minded to regard 'speaking documents', which the griots are, with disdain, and to believe that we know nothing of our past for want of written documents. These men simply prove that they do not know their country except through the eyes of Whites.

The words of traditionist griots deserve anything but scorn. The griot who occupies the chair of history of a village and who bears the title of 'Belen-Tigui' is a very respectable gentleman and has toured Mali. He has gone from village to village to hear the teaching of great masters; he has learnt the art of historical oratory through long years; he is, moreover, bound by an oath and does not teach anything except what his guild stipulates, for, say the griots, 'All true learning should be a secret.' Also the traditionist is a master in the art of circumlocution, he speaks in archaic formulas, or else he turns facts into amusing legends for the public, which legends have, however, a secret sense which the vulgar little suspect.

My eyes have only just opened on these mysteries of eternal Africa and more than once, in my thirst to know, I have had to give up my little claim as an armchair intellectual before the silences of tradition just as my over-impertinent questions were about to uncover a mystery.

This book is, then, the fruit of an initial contact with the most authentic traditionists of Mali. I am nothing more than a translator, I owe everything to the masters of Fadama, Djeliba Koro and Keyla and more particularly to Djeli Mamoudou Kouyaté of the village of Djeliba Koro (Siguiri) in Guinea.

May this book open the eyes of more than one African and induce him to come and sit humbly beside the ancients and hear the words of the griots who teach wisdom and history.

D. T. Niane

The Words of the Griot
Mamadou Kouyaté

I am a griot. It is I, Djeli Mamoudou Kouyaté, son of Bintou Kouyaté and Djeli Kedian Kouyaté, master in the art of eloquence. Since time immemorial the Kouyatés have been in the service of the Keita princes of Mali; we are vessels of speech, we are the repositories which harbour secrets many centuries old. The art of eloquence has no secrets for us; without us the names of kings would vanish into oblivion, we are the memory of mankind; by the spoken word we bring to life the deeds and exploits of kings for younger generations.

I derive my knowledge from my father Djeli Kedian, who also got it from his father; history holds no mystery for us; we teach to the vulgar just as much as we want to teach them, for it is we who keep the keys to the twelve doors of Mali.[1]

I know the list of all the sovereigns who succeeded to the throne of Mali. I know how the black people divided into tribes, for my father bequeathed to me all his learning; I know why such and such is called Kamara, another Keita, and yet another Sibibé or Traoré; every name has a meaning, a secret import.

I teach kings the history of their ancestors so that the lives of the ancients might serve them as an example, for the world is old, but the future springs from the past.

My word is pure and free of all untruth; it is the word of my father; it is the word of my father's father. I will give you my father's words just as I received them; royal griots do not know what lying is. When a quarrel breaks out between tribes it is we who settle the difference, for we are the depositaries of oaths which the ancestors swore.

Listen to my word, you who want to know; by my mouth you will learn the history of Mali.

By my mouth you will get to know the story of the ancestor of great Mali, the story of him who, by his exploits, surpassed even

Alexander the Great; he who, from the East, shed his rays upon all the countries of the West.

Listen to the story of the son of the Buffalo, the son of the Lion.[2] I am going to tell you of Maghan Sundiata, of Mari-Djata, of Sogolon Djata, of Naré Maghan Djata; the man of many names against whom sorcery could avail nothing.

The First Kings of Mali

Listen then, sons of Mali, children of the black people, listen to my word, for I am going to tell you of Sundiata, the father of the Bright Country, of the savanna land, the ancestor of those who draw the bow, the master of a hundred vanquished kings.

I am going to talk of Sundiata, Manding Diara, Lion of Mali, Sogolon Djata, son of Sogolon, Naré Maghan Djata, son of Naré Maghan, Sogo Sogo Simbon Salaba, hero of many names.

I am going to tell you of Sundiata, he whose exploits will astonish men for a long time yet. He was great among kings, he was peerless among men; he was beloved of God because he was the last of the great conquerors.

Right at the beginning then, Mali was a province of the Bambara kings; those who are today called Mandingo,[3] inhabitants of Mali, are not indigenous; they come from the East. Bilali Bounama, ancestor of the Keitas, was the faithful servant of the Prophet Muhammad[4] (may the peace of God be upon him). Bilali Bounama had seven sons of whom the eldest, Lawalo, left the Holy City and came to settle in Mali; Lawalo had Latal Kalabi for a son, Latal Kalabi had Damul Kalabi who then had Lahilatoul Kalabi.

Lahilatoul Kalabi was the first black prince to make the Pilgrimage to Mecca. On his return he was robbed by brigands in the desert; his men were scattered and some died of thirst, but God saved Lahilatoul Kalabi, for he was a righteous man. He called upon the Almighty and jinn appeared and recognized him as king. After seven years' absence Lahilatoul was able to return, by the grace of Allah the Almighty, to Mali where none expected to see him any more.

2

Lahilatoul Kalabi had two sons, the elder being called Kalabi Bomba and the younger Kalabi Dauman; the elder chose royal power and reigned, while the younger preferred fortune and wealth and became the ancestor of those who go from country to country seeking their fortune.

Kalabi Bomba had Mamadi Kani for a son. Mamadi Kani was a hunter king like the first kings of Mali. It was he who invented the hunter's whistle;[5] he communicated with the jinn of the forest and bush. These spirits had no secrets from him and he was loved by Kondolon Ni Sané.[6] His followers were so numerous that he formed them into an army which became formidable; he often gathered them together in the bush and taught them the art of hunting. It was he who revealed to hunters the medicinal leaves which heal wounds and cure diseases. Thanks to the strength of his followers, he became king of a vast country; with them Mamadi Kani conquered all the lands which stretch from the Sankarani to the Bouré. Mamadi Kani had four sons—Kani Simbon, Kamignogo Simbon, Kabala Simbon and Simbon Tagnogokelin. They were all initiated into the art of hunting and deserved the title of Simbon. It was the lineage of Bamari Tagnogokelin which held on to the power; his son was M'Bali Nènè whose son was Bello. Bello's son was called Bello Bakon and he had a son called Maghan Kon Fatta, also called Frako Maghan Keigu, Maghan the handsome.

Maghan Kon Fatta was the father of the great Sundiata and had three wives and six children—three boys and three girls. His first wife was called Sassouma Bérété, daughter of a great divine; she was the mother of King Dankaran Touman and Princess Nana Triban. The second wife, Sogolon Kedjou, was the mother of Sundiata and the two princesses Sogolon Kolonkan and Sogolon Djamarou. The third wife was one of the Kamaras and was called Namandjé; she was the mother of Manding Bory (or Manding Bakary), who was the best friend of his half-brother Sundiata.

The Buffalo Woman

Maghan Kon Fatta, the father of Sundiata, was renowned for his beauty in every land; but he was also a good king loved by all the people. In his capital of Nianiba[7] he loved to sit often at the foot of the great silk-cotton tree[8] which dominated his palace of Canco. Maghan Kon Fatta had been reigning a long time and his eldest son Dankaran Touman was already eight years old and often came to sit on the ox-hide beside his father.

Well now, one day when the king had taken up his usual position under the silk-cotton tree surrounded by his kinsmen he saw a man dressed like a hunter coming towards him; he wore the tight-fitting trousers of the favourites of Kondolon Ni Sané, and his blouse oversewn with cowries showed that he was a master of the hunting art. All present turned towards the unknown man whose bow, polished with frequent usage, shone in the sun. The man walked up in front of the king, whom he recognized in the midst of his courtiers. He bowed and said, 'I salute you, king of Mali, greetings all you of Mali. I am a hunter chasing game and come from Sangaran; a fearless doe has guided me to the walls of Nianiba. By the grace[9] of my master the great Simbon[10] my arrows have hit her and now she lies not far from your walls. As is fitting, oh king, I have come to bring you your portion'. He took a leg from his leather sack whereupon the king's griot, Gnankouman Doua, seized upon the leg and said, 'Stranger, whoever you may be you will be the king's guest because you respect custom; come and take your place on the mat beside us. The king is pleased because he loves righteous men.' The king nodded his approval and all the courtiers agreed. The griot continued in a more familiar tone, 'Oh you who come from the Sangaran, land of the favourites of Kondolon Ni Sané, you who have doubtless had an expert master, will you open your pouch of knowledge for us and instruct us with your conversation, for you have no doubt visited several lands.'

The king, still silent, gave a nod of approval and a courtier added, 'The hunters of Sangaran are the best soothsayers; if the stranger wishes we could learn a lot from him.'

The hunter came and sat down near Gnankouman Doua who vacated one end of the mat to him. Then he said, 'Griot of the king, I am not one of these hunters whose tongues are more dexterous than their arms; I am no spinner of adventure yarns, nor do I like playing upon the credulity of worthy folk; but, thanks to the lore which my master has imparted to me, I can boast of being a seer among seers.'

He took out of his hunter's bag[11] twelve cowries which he threw on the mat. The king and all his entourage now turned towards the stranger who was jumbling up the twelve shiny shells with his bare hand. Gnankouman Doua discreetly brought to the king's notice that the soothsayer was left-handed. The left hand is the hand of evil, but in the divining art it is said that left-handed people are the best. The hunter muttered some incomprehensible words in a low voice while he shuffled and jumbled the twelve cowries into different positions which he mused on at length. All of a sudden he looked up at the king and said, 'Oh king, the world is full of mystery, all is hidden and we know nothing but what we can see. The silk-cotton tree springs from a tiny seed—that which defies the tempest weighs in its germ no more than a grain of rice. Kingdoms are like trees; some will be silk-cotton trees, others will remain dwarf palms and the powerful silk-cotton tree will cover them with its shade. Oh, who can recognize in the little child the great king to come? The great comes from the small; truth and falsehood have both suckled at the same breast. Nothing is certain, but, sire, I can see two strangers over there coming towards your city.'

He fell silent and looked in the direction of the city gates for a short while. All present silently turned towards the gates. The soothsayer returned to his cowries. He shook them in his palm with a skilled hand and then threw them out.

'King of Mali, destiny marches with great strides, Mali is about to emerge from the night. Nianiba is lighting up, but what is this light that comes from the east?'

'Hunter,' said Gnankouman Doua, 'your words are obscure. Make your speech comprehensible to us, speak in the clear language of your savanna.'[12]

'I am coming to that now, griot. Listen to my message. Listen, sire. You have ruled over the kingdom which your ancestors bequeathed to you and you have no other ambition but to pass on this realm, intact if not increased, to your descendants; but, fine king, your successor is not yet born. I see two hunters

5

coming to your city; they have come from afar and a woman accompanies them. Oh, that woman! She is ugly, she is hideous, she bears on her back a disfiguring hump. Her monstrous eyes seem to have been merely laid on her face, but, mystery of mysteries, this is the woman you must marry, sire, for she will be the mother of him who will make the name of Mali immortal for ever. The child will be the seventh star, the seventh conqueror of the earth. He will be more mighty than Alexander. But, oh king, for destiny to lead this woman to you a sacrifice is necessary; you must offer up a red bull, for the bull is powerful. When its blood soaks into the ground nothing more will hinder the arrival of your wife. There, I have said what I had to say, but everything is in the hands of the Almighty.'

The hunter picked up his cowries and put them away in his bag.

'I am only passing through, king of Mali, and now I return to Sangaran. Farewell.'

The hunter disappeared but neither the king, Naré Maghan, nor his griot, Gnankouman Doua, forgot his prophetic words; soothsayers see far ahead, their words are not always for the immediate present; man is in a hurry but time is tardy and everything has its season.

Now one day the king and his suite were again seated under the great silk-cotton tree of Nianiba, chatting as was their wont. Suddenly their gaze was drawn by some strangers who came into the city. The small entourage of the king watched in silent surprise.

Two young hunters, handsome and of fine carriage, were walking along preceded by a young maid. They turned towards the Court. The two men were carrying shining bows of silver on their shoulders. The one who seemed the elder of the two walked with the assurance of a master hunter. When the strangers were a few steps from the king they bowed and the elder spoke thus:

'We greet King Naré Maghan Kon Fatta and his entourage. We come from the land of Do,[13] but my brother and I belong to Mali and we are of the tribe of Traoré. Hunting and adventure led us as far as the distant land of Do where King Mansa Gnemo Diarra reigns. I am called Oulamba and my brother Oulani. The young girl is from Do and we bring her as a present to the king, for my brother and I deemed her worthy to be a king's wife.'

6

The king and his suite tried in vain to get a look at the young girl, for she stayed kneeling, her head lowered, and had deliberately let her kerchief hang in front of her face. If the young girl succeeded in hiding her face, she did not, however, manage to cover up the hump which deformed her shoulders and back. She was ugly in a sturdy sort of way. You could see her muscular arms, and her bulging breasts pushing stoutly against the strong pagne of cotton fabric which was knotted just under her armpit. The king considered her for a moment, then the handsome Maghan turned his head away. He stared a long time at Gnankouman Doua then he lowered his head. The griot understood all the sovereign's embarrassment.

'You are the guests of the king; hunters, we wish you peace in Nianiba, for all the sons of Mali are but one. Come and sit down, slake your thirst and relate to the king by what adventure you left Do with this maiden.'

The king nodded his approval. The two brothers looked at each other and, at a sign from the elder, the younger went up to the king and put down on the ground the calabash of cold water which a servant had brought him.

The hunter said: 'After the great harvest[14] my brother and I left our village to hunt. It was in this way that our pursuit of game led us as far as the approaches of the land of Do. We met two hunters, one of whom was wounded, and we learnt from them that an amazing buffalo was ravaging the countryside of Do. Every day it claimed some victims and nobody dared leave the village after sunset. The king, Do Mansa-Gnemo Diarra, had promised the finest rewards to the hunter who killed the buffalo. We decided to try our luck too and so we penetrated into the land of Do. We were advancing warily, our eyes well skinned, when we saw an old woman by the side of a river. She was weeping and lamenting, gnawed by hunger. Until then no passer-by had deigned to stop by her. She beseeched us, in the name of the Almighty, to give her something to eat. Touched by her tears I approached and took some pieces of dried meat from my hunter's bag. When she had eaten well she said, "Hunter, may God requite you with the charity you have given me." We were making ready to leave when she stopped me. "I know," she said, "that you are going to try your luck against the Buffalo of Do, but you should know that many others before you have met their

7

death through their foolhardiness, for arrows are useless against the buffalo; but, young hunter, your heart is generous and it is you who will be the buffalo's vanquisher. I am the buffalo you are looking for, and your generosity has vanquished me. I am the buffalo that ravages Do. I have killed a hundred and seven hunters and wounded seventy-seven; every day I kill an inhabitant of Do and the king, Gnemo Diarra, is at his wit's end which jinn to sacrifice to. Here, young man, take this distaff and this egg and go to the plain of Ourantamba where I browse among the king's crops. Before using your bow you must take aim at me three times with this distaff; then draw your bow and I shall be vulnerable to your arrow. I shall fall but shall get up and pursue you into a dry plain. Then throw the egg behind you and a great mire will come into being where I shall be unable to advance and then you will kill me. As a proof of your victory you must cut off the buffalo's tail, which is of gold, and take it to the king, from whom you will exact your due reward. As for me, I have run my course and punished the king of Do, my brother, for depriving me of my part of the inheritance." Crazy with joy, I seized the distaff and the egg, but the old woman stopped me with a gesture and said, "There is one condition, hunter." "What condition?" I replied impatiently. "The king promises the hand of the most beautiful maiden of Do to the victor. When all the people of Do are gathered and you are told to choose her whom you want as a wife you must search in the crowd and you will find a very ugly maid—uglier than you can imagine—sitting apart on an observation platform; it is her you must choose. She is called Sogolon Kedjou, or Sogolon Kondouto, because she is a hunchback. You will choose her for she is my wraith.[15] She will be an extraordinary woman if you manage to possess her. Promise me you will choose her, hunter." I swore to, solemnly, between the hands of the old woman, and we continued on our way. The plain of Ourantamba was half a day's journey from there. On the way we saw hunters who were fleeing and who watched us quite dumbfounded. The buffalo was at the other end of the plain but when it saw us it charged with menacing horns. I did as the old woman had told me and killed the buffalo. I cut off its tail and we went back to the town of Do as night was falling, but we did not go before the king until morning came.[16] The king had the drums beaten and before midday all the inhabitants of the country were gathered in the main square. The mutilated carcass of the buffalo had been placed in the middle of the square and the delirious crowd abused it, while our names were sung in a thousand refrains. When the king appeared a deep silence settled on the crowd. "I promised the hand of the most beautiful maiden in Do to the brave hunter who saved us from the scourge which overwhelmed us. The buffalo of Do is dead and here is the hunter who has killed it. I am a man of my word. Hunter, here are all the daughters of Do; take your pick." And the crowd showed its approval by a great cheer. On that day all the daughters of Do wore their festive dress; gold shone in their hair and fragile wrists bent under the weight of heavy silver bracelets. Never did so much beauty come together in one place. Full of pride, my quiver on my back, I swaggered before the beautiful girls of Do who were smiling at me, with their teeth as white as the rice of Mali. But I remembered the words of the old woman. I went round the great circle many times until at last I saw Sogolon Kedjou sitting apart on a raised platform. I elbowed my way through the crowd, took Sogolon by the hand and drew her into the middle of the circle. Showing her to the king, I said, "Oh King Gnemo Diarra, here is the one I have chosen from among the young maids of Do; it is her I would like for a wife." The choice was so paradoxical that the king could not help laughing, and then general laughter broke out and the people split their sides with mirth. They took me for a fool, and I became a ludicrous hero. "You've got to belong to the tribe of Traoré to do things like that," said somebody in the crowd, and it was thus that my brother and I left Do the very same day pursued by the mockery of the Kondés.'[17]

The hunter ended his story and the noble king Naré Maghan determined to solemnize his marriage with all the customary formalities so that nobody could dispute the rights of the son to be born to him. The two hunters were considered as being relatives of Sogolon and it was to them that Gnankouman Doua bore the traditional cola nuts.[18] By agreement with the hunters the marriage was fixed for the first Wednesday of the new moon. The twelve villages of old Mali and all the peoples allied to them were acquainted with this and on the appointed day delegations flocked from all sides to Nianiba, the town of Maghan Kon Fatta.

Sogolon had been lodged with an old aunt of the king's. Since her arrival in Nianiba she had never once gone out and everyone longed to see the woman for whom Naré Maghan was preparing such a magnificent wedding. It was known that she was not beautiful, but the curiosity of everyone was aroused, and already a thousand anecdotes were circulating, most of them put about by Sassouma Bérété, the king's first wife.

The royal drums of Nianiba announced the festivity at crack of dawn. The town awoke to the sound of tam-tams which answered each other from one district to another; from the midst of the crowds arose the voices of griots singing the praises of Naré Maghan.

At the home of the king's old aunt, the hairdresser of Nianiba was plaiting Sogolon Kedjou's hair. As she lay on her mat, her head resting on the hairdresser's legs, she wept softly, while the king's sisters came to chaff her, as was the custom.

'This is your last day of freedom; from now onwards you will be our woman.'

'Say farewell to your youth,' added another.

'You won't dance in the square any more and have yourself admired by the boys,' added a third.

Sogolon never uttered a word and from time to time the old hairdresser said, 'There, there, stop crying. It's a new life beginning, you know, more beautiful than you think. You will be a mother and you will know the joy of being a queen surrounded by your children. Come now, daughter, don't listen to the gibes of your sisters-in-law.' In front of the house the poetesses who belonged to the king's sisters chanted the name of the young bride.

During this time the festivity was reaching its height in front of the king's enclosure. Each village was represented by a troupe of dancers and musicians; in the middle of the courtyard the elders were sacrificing oxen which the servants carved up, while ungainly vultures, perched on the great silk-cotton tree, watched the hecatomb with their eyes.

Sitting in front of the palace, Naré Maghan listened to the grave music of the 'bolon'[19] in the midst of his courtiers. Doua, standing amid the eminent guests, held his great spear in his hand and sang the anthem of the Mandingo kings. Everywhere in the village people were dancing and singing and members of the royal family evinced their joy, as was fitting, by distributing

10

grain, clothes, and even gold. Even the jealous Sassouma Bérété took part in this largesse and, among other things, bestowed fine loin-cloths on the poetesses.

But night was falling and the sun had hidden behind the mountain. It was time for the marriage procession to form up in front of the house of the king's aunt. The tam-tams had fallen silent. The old female relatives of the king had washed and perfumed Sogolon and now she was dressed completely in white with a large veil over her head.

Sogolon walked in front held by two old women. The king's relatives followed and, behind, the choir of young girls of Mali sang the bride's departure song, keeping time to the songs by clapping their hands. The villagers and guests were lined up along the stretch of ground which separated the aunt's house from the palace in order to see the procession go by. When Sogolon had reached the threshold of the king's antechamber one of his young brothers lifted her vigorously from the ground and ran off with her towards the palace while the crowd cheered.

The women danced in front of the palace of the king for a long while, then, after receiving money and presents from members of the royal family, the crowd dispersed and night darkened overhead.

'She will be an extraordinary woman if you manage to possess her.' Those were the words of the old woman of Do, but the conqueror of the buffalo had not been able to conquer the young girl. It was only as an afterthought that the two hunters, Oulani and Oulamba, had the idea of giving her to the king of Mali.

That evening, then, Naré Maghan tried to perform his duty as a husband but Sogolon repulsed his advances. He persisted, but his efforts were in vain and early the next morning Doua found the king exhausted, like a man who had suffered a great defeat.

'What is the matter, my king?' asked the griot.

'I have been unable to possess her—and besides, she frightens me, this young girl. I even doubt whether she is a human being; when I drew close to her during the night her body became covered with long hairs and that scared me very much. All night long I called upon my wraith but he was unable to master Sogolon's.'

All that day the king did not emerge and Doua was the only one to enter and leave the palace. All Nianiba seemed puzzled. The old women who had come early to seek the virginity pagne[20] had been discreetly turned away. And this went on for a week.

Naré Maghan had vainly sought advice from some great sorcerers but all their tricks were powerless in overcoming the wraith of Sogolon. But one night, when everyone was asleep, Naré Maghan got up. He unhooked his hunter's bag from the wall and, sitting in the middle of the house, he spread on the ground the sand which the bag contained. The king began tracing mysterious signs in the sand; he traced, effaced and began again. Sogolon woke up. She knew that sand talks,[21] but she was intrigued to see the king so absorbed at dead of night. Naré Maghan stopped drawing signs and with his hand under his chin he seemed to be brooding on the signs. All of a sudden he jumped up, bounded after his sword which hung above his bed, and said, 'Sogolon, Sogolon, wake up. A dream has awakened me out of my sleep and the protective spirit of the Mandingo kings has appeared to me. I was mistaken in the interpretation I put upon the words of the hunter who led you to me. The jinn has revealed to me their real meaning. Sogolon, I must sacrifice you to the greatness of my house. The blood of a virgin of the tribe of Kondé must be spilt, and you are the Kondé virgin whom fate has brought under my roof. Forgive me, but I must accomplish my mission. Forgive the hand which is going to shed your blood.'

'No, no—why me?—no, I don't want to die.'

'It is useless,' said the king. 'It is not me who has decided.'

He seized Sogolon by the hair with an iron grip, but so great had been her fright that she had already fainted. In this faint, she was congealed in her human body and her wraith was no longer in her, and when she woke up, she was already a wife. That very night, Sogolon conceived.[22]

The Lion Child

A wife quickly grows accustomed to her state. Sogolon now walked freely in the king's great enclosure and people also got used to her ugliness. But the first wife of the king, Sassouma Bérété, turned out to be unbearable. She was restless, and smarted to see the ugly Sogolon proudly flaunting her pregnancy about the palace. What would become of her, Sassouma Bérété, if her son, already eight years old, was disinherited in favour of the child that Sogolon was going to bring into the world? All the king's attentions went to the mother-to-be. On returning from the wars he would bring her the best portion of the booty—fine loin-cloths and rare jewels. Soon, dark schemes took form in the mind of Sassouma Bérété; she determined to kill Sogolon. In great secrecy she had the foremost sorcerers of Mali come to her, but they all declared themselves incapable of tackling Sogolon. In fact, from twilight onwards, three owls[23] came and perched on the roof of her house and watched over her. For the sake of peace and quiet Sassouma said to herself, 'Very well then, let him be born, this child, and then we'll see.''

Sogolon's time came. The king commanded the nine greatest midwives of Mali to come to Niani, and they were now constantly in attendance on the damsel of Do. The king was in the midst of his courtiers one day when someone came to announce to him that Sogolon's labours were beginning. He sent all his courtiers away and only Gnankouman Doua stayed by his side. One would have thought that this was the first time that he had become a father, he was so worried and agitated. The whole palace kept complete silence. Doua tried to distract the sovereign with his one-stringed guitar but in vain. He even had to stop this music as it jarred on the king. Suddenly the sky darkened and great clouds coming from the east hid the sun, although it was still the dry season. Thunder began to rumble and swift lightning rent the clouds; a few large drops of rain began to fall while a strong wind blew up. A flash of lightning accompanied by a dull rattle of thunder burst out of the east and lit up the whole sky as far as the west. Then the rain stopped and the sun appeared and it was at this very moment that a midwife came out of Sogolon's house, ran to the antechamber and announced to Naré Maghan that he was the father of a boy.

The king showed no reaction at all. He was as though in a daze. Then Doua, realizing the king's emotion, got up and signalled to two slaves who were already standing near the royal 'tabala'.[24] The hasty beats of the royal drum announced to Mali the birth of a son; the village tam-tams took it up and thus all Mali got the good news the same day. Shouts of joy, tam-tams and 'balafons'[25] took the place of the recent silence and all the musicians of Niani made their way to the palace. His initial emotion being over, the king had got up and on leaving the antechamber he was greeted by the warm voice of Gnankouman Doua singing:

'I salute you, father; I salute you, king Naré Maghan; I salute you, Maghan Kon Fatta, Frako Maghan Keigu.[26] The child is born whom the world awaited. Maghan, oh happy father, I salute you. The lion child, the buffalo child is born, and to announce him the Almighty has made the thunder peal, the whole sky has lit up and the earth has trembled. All hail, father, hail king Naré Maghan!'

All the griots were there and had already composed a song in praise of the royal infant. The generosity of kings makes griots eloquent, and Maghan Kon Fatta distributed on this day alone six granaries of rice among the populace. Sassouma Bérété distinguished herself by her largesses, but that deceived nobody. She was suffering in her heart but did not want to betray anything.

The name was given the eighth day after his birth. It was a great feast day and people came from all the villages of Mali while each neighbouring people brought gifts to the king. First thing in the morning a great circle had formed in front of the palace. In the middle, serving women were pounding rice which was to serve as bread, and sacrificed oxen lay at the foot of the great silk-cotton tree.

In Sogolon's house the king's aunt cut off the baby's first crop of hair while the poetesses, equipped with large fans, cooled the mother who was nonchalantly stretched out on soft cushions.

The king was in his antechamber but he came out followed by Doua. The crowd fell silent and Doua cried, 'The child of Sogolon will be called Maghan after his father, and Mari Djata, a name which no Mandingo prince has ever borne. Sogolon's son will be the first of this name."

Straight away the griots shouted the name of the infant and the tam-tams sounded anew. The king's aunt, who had come out to hear the name of the child, went back into the house, and whispered the double name of Maghan and Mari Djata in the ear of the newly-born so that he would remember it.

The festivity ended with the distribution of meat to the heads of families and everyone dispersed joyfully. The near relatives one by one went to admire the newly-born.

Childhood

God has his mysteries which none can fathom. You, perhaps, will be a king. You can do nothing about it. You, on the other hand, will be unlucky, but you can do nothing about that either. Each man finds his way already marked out for him and he can change nothing of it.

Sogolon's son had a slow and difficult childhood. At the age of three he still crawled along on all-fours while children of the same age were already walking. He had nothing of the great beauty of his father Naré Maghan. He had a head so big that he seemed unable to support it; he also had large eyes which would open wide whenever anyone entered his mother's house. He was taciturn and used to spend the whole day just sitting in the middle of the house. Whenever his mother went out he would crawl on all fours to rummage about in the calabashes in search of food, for he was very greedy.[27]

Malicious tongues began to blab. What three-year-old has not yet taken his first steps? What three-year-old is not the despair of his parents through his whims and shifts of mood? What three-year-old is not the joy of his circle through his backwardness in talking? Sogolon Djata (for it was thus that they called him, prefixing his mother's name to his), Sogolon Djata, then, was very different from others of his own age. He spoke little and his severe face never relaxed into a smile. You would have thought that he was already thinking, and what amused children of his age bored him. Often Sogolon would make some of them come to him to keep him company. These children were already walking and she hoped that Djata, seeing his companions walking, would be tempted to do likewise. But nothing came of it. Besides, Sogolon Djata would brain the poor little things with his already strong arms and none of them would come near him any more.

The king's first wife was the first to rejoice at Sogolon Djata's infirmity. Her own son, Dankaran Touman, was already eleven. He was a fine and lively boy, who spent the day running about the village with those of his own age. He had even begun his initiation in the bush.[28] The king had had a bow made for him and he used to go behind the town to practise archery with his companions. Sassouma was quite happy and snapped her fingers at Sogolon, whose child was still crawling on the ground. Whenever the latter happened to pass by her house, she would say, 'Come, my son, walk, jump, leap about. The jinn didn't promise you anything out of the ordinary, but I prefer a son who walks on his two legs to a lion that crawls on the ground.' She spoke thus whenever Sogolon went by her door. The innuendo would go straight home and then she would burst into laughter, that diabolical laughter which a jealous woman knows how to use so well.

Her son's infirmity weighed heavily upon Sogolon Kedjou; she had resorted to all her talent as a sorceress to give strength to her son's legs, but the rarest herbs had been useless. The king himself lost hope.

How impatient man is! Naré Maghan became imperceptibly estranged but Gnankouman Doua never ceased reminding him of the hunter's words. Sogolon became pregnant again. The king hoped for a son, but it was a daughter called Kolonkan. She resembled her mother and had nothing of her father's beauty. The disheartened king debarred Sogolon from his house and she lived in semi-disgrace for a while. Naré Maghan married the daughter of one of his allies, the king of the Kamaras. She was called Namandjé and her beauty was legendary. A year later she brought a boy into the world. When the king consulted soothsayers on the destiny of this son he received the reply that Namandjé's child would be the right hand of some mighty king. The king gave the newly-born the name of Boukari. He was to be called Manding Boukari or Manding Bory later on.

Naré Maghan was very perplexed. Could it be that the stiff-jointed son of Sogolon was the one the hunter soothsayer had foretold?

'The Almighty has his mysteries,' Gnankouman Doua would say and, taking up the hunter's words, added, 'The silk-cotton tree emerges from a tiny seed.'

16

One day Naré Maghan came along to the house of Nounfaïri, the blacksmith seer of Niani. He was an old, blind man. He received the king in the anteroom which served as his workshop. To the king's question he replied, 'When the seed germinates growth is not always easy; great trees grow slowly but they plunge their roots deep into the ground.'

'But has the seed really germinated?' said the king.

'Of course,' replied the blind seer. 'Only the growth is not as quick as you would like it; how impatient man is.'

This interview and Doua's confidence gave the king some assurance. To the great displeasure of Sassouma Bérété the king restored Sogolon to favour and soon another daughter was born to her. She was given the name of Djamarou.

However, all Niani talked of nothing else but the stiff-legged son of Sogolon. He was now seven and he still crawled to get about. In spite of all the king's affection, Sogolon was in despair. Naré Maghan aged and he felt his time coming to an end. Dankaran Touman, the son of Sassouma Bérété, was now a fine youth.

One day Naré Maghan made Mari Djata come to him and he spoke to the child as one speaks to an adult. 'Mari Djata, I am growing old and soon I shall be no more among you, but before death takes me off I am going to give you the present each king gives his successor. In Mali every prince has his own griot. Doua's father was my father's griot, Doua is mine and the son of Doua, Balla Fasséké here, will be your griot. Be inseparable friends from this day forward. From his mouth you will hear the history of your ancestors, you will learn the art of governing Mali according to the principles which our ancestors have bequeathed to us. I have served my term and done my duty too. I have done everything which a king of Mali ought to do. I am handing an enlarged kingdom over to you and I leave you sure allies. May your destiny be accomplished, but never forget that Niani is your capital and Mali the cradle of your ancestors.'

The child, as if he had understood the whole meaning of the king's words, beckoned Balla Fasséké to approach. He made room for him on the hide he was sitting on and then said, 'Balla, you will be my griot.'

'Yes, son of Sogolon, if it pleases God,' replied Balla Fasséké.

The king and Doua exchanged glances that radiated confidence.

The Lion's Awakening

A short while after this interview between Naré Maghan and his son the king died. Sogolon's son was no more than seven years old. The council of elders met in the king's palace. It was no use Doua's defending the king's will which reserved the throne for Mari Djata, for the council took no account of Naré Maghan's wish. With the help of Sassouma Bérété's intrigues, Dankaran Touman was proclaimed king and a regency council was formed in which the queen mother was all-powerful. A short time after, Doua died.

As men have short memories, Sogolon's son was spoken of with nothing but irony and scorn. People had seen one-eyed kings, one-armed kings, and lame kings, but a stiff-legged king had never been heard tell of. No matter how great the destiny promised for Mari Djata might be, the throne could not be given to someone who had no power in his legs; if the jinn loved him, let them begin by giving him the use of his legs. Such were the remarks that Sogolon heard every day. The queen mother, Sassouma Bérété, was the source of all this gossip.

Having become all-powerful, Sassouma Bérété persecuted Sogolon because the late Naré Maghan had preferred her. She banished Sogolon and her son to a back yard of the palace. Mari Djata's mother now occupied an old hut which had served as a lumber-room of Sassouma's.

The wicked queen mother allowed free passage to all those inquisitive people who wanted to see the child that still crawled at the age of seven. Nearly all the inhabitants of Niani filed into the palace and the poor Sogolon wept to see herself thus given over to public ridicule. Mari Djata took on a ferocious look in front of the crowd of sightseers. Sogolon found a little consolation only in the love of her eldest daughter, Kolonkan. She was four and she could walk. She seemed to understand all her mother's miseries and already she helped her with the housework. Sometimes, when Sogolon was attending to the chores, it was she who stayed beside her sister Djamarou, quite small as yet.

Sogolon Kedjou and her children lived on the queen mother's left-overs, but she kept a little garden in the open ground behind the village. It was there that she passed her brightest moments

18

looking after her onions and gnougous.[29] One day she happened to be short of condiments and went to the queen mother to beg a little baobab leaf.[30]

'Look you,' said the malicious Sassouma, 'I have a calabash full. Help yourself, you poor woman. As for me, my son knew how to walk at seven and it was he who went and picked these baobab leaves. Take them then, since your son is unequal to mine.' Then she laughed derisively with that fierce laughter which cuts through your flesh and penetrates right to the bone.

Sogolon Kedjou was dumbfounded. She had never imagined that hate could be so strong in a human being. With a lump in her throat she left Sassouma's. Outside her hut Mari Djata, sitting on his useless legs, was blandly eating out of a calabash. Unable to contain herself any longer, Sogolon burst into sobs and seizing a piece of wood, hit her son.

'Oh son of misfortune, will you never walk? Through your fault I have just suffered the greatest affront of my life! What have I done, God, for you to punish me in this way?'

Mari Djata seized the piece of wood and, looking at his mother, said, 'Mother, what's the matter?'

'Shut up, nothing can ever wash me clean of this insult.'

'But what then?'

'Sassouma has just humiliated me over a matter of a baobab leaf. At your age her own son could walk and used to bring his mother baobab leaves.''

'Cheer up, Mother, cheer up.'

'No. It's too much. I can't.'

'Very well then, I am going to walk today,' said Mari Djata. 'Go and tell my father's smiths to make me the heaviest possible iron rod. Mother, do you want just the leaves of the baobab or would you rather I brought you the whole tree?'

'Ah, my son, to wipe out this insult I want the tree and its roots at my feet outside my hut.'

Balla Fasséké, who was present, ran to the master smith, Farakourou, to order an iron rod.

Sogolon had sat down in front of her hut. She was weeping softly and holding her head between her two hands. Mari Djata went calmly back to his calabash of rice and began eating again as if nothing had happened. From time to time he looked up discreetly at his mother who was murmuring in a low voice,

'I want the whole tree, in front of my hut, the whole tree.'

All of a sudden a voice burst into laughter behind the hut. It was the wicked Sassouma telling one of her serving women about the scene of humiliation and she was laughing loudly so that Sogolon could hear. Sogolon fled into the hut and hid her face under the blankets so as not to have before her eyes this heedless boy, who was more preoccupied with eating than with anything else. With her head buried in the bed-clothes Sogolon wept and her body shook violently. Her daughter, Sogolon Djamarou, had come and sat down beside her and she said, 'Mother, Mother, don't cry. Why are you crying?'

Mari Djata had finished eating and, dragging himself along on his legs, he came and sat under the wall of the hut for the sun was scorching. What was he thinking about? He alone knew.

The royal forges were situated outside the walls and over a hundred smiths worked there. The bows, spears, arrows and shields of Niani's warriors came from there. When Balla Fasséké came to order the iron rod, Farakourou said to him, 'The great day has arrived then?'

'Yes. Today is a day like any other, but it will see what no other day has seen.'

The master of the forges, Farakourou, was the son of the old Nounfaïri, and he was a soothsayer like his father. In his workshops there was an enormous iron bar wrought by his father Nounfaïri. Everybody wondered what this bar was destined to be used for. Farakourou called six of his apprentices and told them to carry the iron bar to Sogolon's house.

When the smiths put the gigantic iron bar down in front of the hut the noise was so frightening that Sogolon, who was lying down, jumped up with a start. Then Balla Fasséké, son of Gnankouman Doua, spoke.

'Here is the great day, Mari Djata. I am speaking to you, Maghan, son of Sogolon. The waters of the Niger can efface the stain from the body, but they cannot wipe out an insult. Arise, young lion, roar, and may the bush know that from henceforth it has a master.'

The apprentice smiths were still there, Sogolon had come out and everyone was watching Mari Djata. He crept on all-fours and came to the iron bar. Supporting himself on his knees and one hand, with the other hand he picked up the iron bar without any effort and stood it up vertically. Now he was resting on nothing but his knees and held the bar with both his hands. A deathly silence had gripped all those present. Sogolon Djata closed his eyes, held tight, the muscles in his arms tensed. With a violent jerk he threw his weight on to it and his knees left the ground. Sogolon Kedjou was all eyes and watched her son's legs which were trembling as though from an electric shock. Djata was sweating and the sweat ran from his brow. In a great effort he straightened up and was on his feet at one go—but the great bar of iron was twisted and had taken the form of a bow!

Then Balla Fasséké sang out the 'Hymn to the Bow', striking up with his powerful voice:

> 'Take your bow, Simbon,
> Take your bow and let us go.
> Take your bow, Sogolon Djata.'

When Sogolon saw her son standing she stood dumb for a moment, then suddenly she sang these words of thanks to God who had given her son the use of his legs:

> 'Oh day, what a beautiful day,
> Oh day, day of joy;
> Allah Almighty, you never created a finer day.
> So my son is going to walk!'

Standing in the position of a soldier at ease, Sogolon Djata, supported by his enormous rod, was sweating great beads of sweat. Balla Fasséké's song had alerted the whole palace and people came running from all over to see what had happened, and each stood bewildered before Sogolon's son. The queen mother had rushed there and when she saw Mari Djata standing up she trembled from head to foot. After recovering his breath Sogolon's son dropped the bar and the crowd stood to one side. His first steps were those of a giant. Balla Fasséké fell into step and pointing his finger at Djata, he cried:

> 'Room, room, make room!
> The lion has walked;
> Hide antelopes,
> Get out of his way.'

Behind Niani there was a young baobab tree and it was there that the children of the town came to pick leaves for their mothers. With all his might the son of Sogolon tore up the tree and put it on his shoulders and went back to his mother. He threw the tree in front of the hut and said, 'Mother, here are some baobab leaves for you. From henceforth it will be outside your hut that the women of Niani will come to stock up.'

Sogolon Djata walked. From that day forward the queen mother had no more peace of mind. But what can one do against destiny? Nothing. Man, under the influence of certain illusions, thinks he can alter the course which God has mapped out, but everything he does falls into a higher order which he barely understands. That is why Sassouma's efforts were vain against Sogolon's son, everything she did lay in the child's destiny. Scorned the day before and the object of public ridicule, now Sogolon's son was as popular as he had been despised. The multitude loves and fears strength. All Niani talked of nothing but Djata; the mothers urged their sons to become hunting companions of Djata and to share his games, as if they wanted their offspring to profit from the nascent glory of the buffalo-woman's son. The words of Doua on the name-giving day came back to men's minds and Sogolon was now surrounded with much respect; in conversation people were fond of contrasting Sogolon's modesty with the pride and malice of Soussouma Bérété. It was because the former had been an exemplary wife and mother that God had granted strength to her son's legs for, it was said, the more a wife loves and respects her husband and the more she suffers for her child, the more valorous will the child be one day. Each is the child of his mother; the child is worth no more than the mother is worth. It was not astonishing that the king Dankaran Touman was so colourless, for his mother had never shown the slightest respect to her husband and never, in the presence of the late king, did she show that humility which every wife should show before her husband. People recalled her scenes of jealousy and the spiteful remarks she circulated about her co-wife and her child. And people would conclude gravely, 'Nobody knows God's mystery. The snake has no legs yet it is as swift as any other animal that has four.'

Sogolon Djata's popularity grew from day to day and he was surrounded by a gang of children of the same age as himself.

These were Fran Kamara, son of the king of Tabon; Kamandjan, son of the king of Sibi; and other princes whose fathers had sent them to the court of Niani.[31] The son of Namandjé, Manding Bory, was already joining in their games. Balla Fasséké followed Sogolon Djata all the time. He was past twenty and it was he who gave the child education and instruction according to Mandingo rules of conduct. Whether in town or at the hunt, he missed no opportunity of instructing his pupil. Many young boys of Niani came to join in the games of the royal child.

He liked hunting best of all. Farakourou, master of the forges, had made Djata a fine bow, and he proved himself to be a good shot with the bow. He made frequent hunting trips with his troops, and in the evening all Niani would be in the square to be present at the entry of the young hunters. The crowd would sing the 'Hymn to the Bow' which Balla Fasséké had composed, and Sogolon Djata was quite young when he received the title of Simbon, or master hunter, which is only conferred on great hunters who have proved themselves.

Every evening Sogolon Kedjou would gather Djata and his companions outside her hut. She would tell them stories about the beasts of the bush, the dumb brothers of man. Sogolon Djata learnt to distinguish between the animals; he knew why the buffalo was his mother's wraith and also why the lion was the protector of his father's family. He also listened to the history of the kings which Balla Fasséké told him; enraptured by the story of Alexander the Great,[32] the mighty king of gold and silver, whose sun shone over quite half the world. Sogolon initiated her son into certain secrets and revealed to him the names of the medicinal plants which every hunter should know. Thus, between his mother and his griot, the child got to know all that needed to be known.

Sogolon's son was now ten. The name Sogolon Djata in the rapid Mandingo language became Sundiata or Sondjata. He was a lad full of strength; his arms had the strength of ten and his biceps inspired fear in his companions. He had already that authoritative way of speaking which belongs to those who are destined to command. His brother, Manding Bory, became his best friend, and whenever Djata was seen, Manding Bory appeared too. They were like a man and his shadow. Fran Kamara and Kamandjan were the closest friends of the young princes, while Balla Fasséké followed them all like a guardian angel.

But Sundiata's popularity was so great that the queen mother became apprehensive for her son's throne. Dankaran Touman was the most retiring of men. At the age of eighteen he was still under the influence of his mother and a handful of old schemers. It was Sassouma Bérété who really reigned in his name. The queen mother wanted to put an end to this popularity by killing Sundiata and it was thus that one night she received the nine great witches of Mali. They were all old women. The eldest, and the most dangerous too, was called Soumosso Konkomba. When the nine old hags had seated themselves in a semi-circle around her bed the queen mother said:

'You who rule supreme at night, nocturnal powers, oh you who hold the secret of life, you who can put an end to one life, can you help me?'

'The night is potent,' said Soumosso Konkomba, 'Oh queen, tell us what is to be done, on whom must we turn the fatal blade?'

'I want to kill Sundiata,' said Sassouma. 'His destiny runs counter to my son's and he must be killed while there is still time. If you succeed, I promise you the finest rewards. First of all I bestow on each of you a cow and her calf and from tomorrow go to the royal granaries and each of you will receive a hundred measures of rice and a hundred measures of hay on my authority.'

'Mother of the king,' rejoined Soumosso Konkomba, 'life hangs by nothing but a very fine thread, but all is interwoven here below. Life has a cause, and death as well. The one comes from the other. Your hate has a cause and your action must have a cause. Mother of the king, everything holds together, our action will have no effect unless we are ourselves implicated, but Mari Djata has done us no wrong. It is, then, difficult for us to compass his death.'

'But you are also concerned,' replied the queen mother, 'for the son of Sogolon will be a scourge to us all.'

'The snake seldom bites the foot that does not walk,' said one of the witches.

'Yes, but there are snakes that attack everybody. Allow Sundiata to grow up and we will all repent of it. Tomorrow go to Sogolon's vegetable patch and make a show of picking a few gnougou leaves. Mari Djata stands guard there and you will see how vicious the boy is. He won't have any respect for your age, he'll give you a good thrashing.'

'That's a clever idea,' said one of the old hags.

'But the cause of our discomfiture will be ourselves, for having touched something which did not belong to us.'

'We could repeat the offence,' said another, 'and then if he beats us again we would be able to reproach him with being unkind, heartless. In that case we would be concerned, I think.'

'The idea is ingenious,' said Soumosso Konkomba. 'Tomorrow we shall go to Sogolon's vegetable patch.'

'Now there's.a happy thought,' concluded the queen mother, laughing for joy. 'Go to the vegetable patch tomorrow and you will see that Sogolon's son is mean. Beforehand, present yourselves at the royal granaries where you will receive the grain I promised you; the cows and calves are already yours.'

The old hags bowed and disappeared into the black night. The queen mother was now alone and gloated over her anticipated victory. But her daughter, Nana Triban, woke up.

'Mother, who were you talking to? I thought I heard voices.'

'Sleep, my daughter, it is nothing. You didn't hear anything.'

In the morning, as usual, Sundiata got his companions together in front of his mother's hut and said, 'What animal are we going to hunt today?'

Kamandjan said, 'I wouldn't mind if we attacked some elephants right now.'

'Yes, I am of this opinion too,' said Fran Kamara. 'That will allow us to go far into the bush.'

And the young band left after Sogolon had filled the hunting bags with eatables. Sundiata and his companions came back late to the village, but first Djata wanted to take a look at his mother's vegetable patch as was his custom. It was dusk. There he found the nine witches stealing gnougou leaves. They made a show of running away like thieves caught red-handed.

'Stop, stop, poor old women,' said Sundiata, 'what is the matter with you to run away like this. This garden belongs to all.'

Straight away his companions and he filled the gourds of the old hags with leaves, aubergines and onions.

'Each time that you run short of condiments come to stock up here without fear.'

'You disarm us,' said one of the old crones, and another added, 'And you confound us with your bounty.'

'Listen, Djata,' said Soumosso Konkomba, 'we had come here to test you. We have no need of condiments but your generosity disarms us. We were sent here by the queen mother to provoke you and draw the anger of the nocturnal powers upon you. But nothing can be done against a heart full of kindness. And to think that we have already drawn a hundred measures of rice and a hundred measures of millet[33]—and the queen promises us each a cow and her calf in addition. Forgive us, son of Sogolon.'

'I bear you no ill-will,' said Djata. 'Here, I am returning from the hunt with my companions and we have killed ten elephants, so I will give you an elephant each and there you have some meat!'

'Thank you, son of Sogolon.'

'Thank you, child of Justice.'

'Henceforth,' concluded Soumosso Konkomba, 'we will watch over you.' And the nine witches disappeared into the night. Sundiata and his companions continued on their way to Niani and got back after dark.

'You were really frightened; those nine witches really scared you, eh?' said Sogolon Kolonkan, Djata's young sister.

'How do you know,' retorted Sundiata, astonished.

'I saw them at night hatching their scheme, but I knew there was no danger for you.' Kolonkan was well versed in the art of witchcraft and watched over her brother without his suspecting it.

Exile

But Sogolon was a wise mother. She knew everything that Sassouma could do to hurt her family, and so, one evening, after the children had eaten, she called them together and said to Sundiata.

'Let us leave here, my son; Manding Bory and Djamarou are vulnerable. They are not yet initiated into the secrets of night, they are not sorcerers. Despairing of ever injuring you, Sassouma will aim her blows at your brother or sister. Let us go away from here. You will return to reign when you are a man, for it is in Mali that your destiny must be fulfilled.'

It was the wisest course. Manding Bory, the son of Naré Maghan's third wife, Namandjé, had no gift of sorcery. Sundiata loved him very much and since the death of Namandjé he had been welcomed by Sogolon. Sundiata had found a great friend in his half-brother. You cannot choose your relatives but you can choose your friends. Manding Bory and Sundiata were real friends and it was to save his brother that Djata accepted exile.

Balla Fasséké, Djata's griot, prepared the departure in detail. But Sassouma Bérété kept her eye on Sogolon and her family.

One morning the king, Dankaran Touman, called the council together. He announced his intention of sending an embassy to the powerful king of Sosso, Soumaoro Kanté. For such a delicate mission he had thought of Balla Fasséké, son of Doua, his father's griot. The council approved the royal decision, the embassy was formed and Balla Fasséké was at the head of it.

It was a very clever way of taking away from Sundiata the griot his father had given him. Djata was out hunting and when he came back in the evening, Sogolon Kedjou told him the news. The embassy had left that very morning. Sundiata flew into a frightful rage.

'What! take away the griot my father gave me! No, he will give me back my griot.'

'Stop!' said Sogolon. 'Let it go. It is Sassouma who is acting thus, but she does not know that she obeys a higher order.'

'Come with me,' said Sundiata to his brother Manding Bory, and the two princes went out. Djata bundled aside the guards on the house of Dankaran Touman, but he was so angry that he could not utter a word. It was Manding Bory who spoke.

'Brother Dankaran Touman, you have taken away our part of the inheritance. Every prince has had his griot, and you have taken away Balla Fasséké. He was not yours but wherever he may be, Balla will always be Djata's griot. And since you do not want to have us around you we shall leave Mali and go far away from here.'

'But I will return,' added the son of Sogolon, vehemently. 'I will return, do you hear?'

'You know that you are going away but you do not know if you will come back,' the king replied.

27

'I *will* return, do you hear me?' Djata went on and his tone was categorical. A shiver ran through the king's whole body. Dankaran Touman trembled in every limb. The two princes went out. The queen mother hurried in and found her son in a state of collapse.

'Mother, he is leaving but he says he will return. But why is he leaving? I intend to give him back his griot, for my part. Why is he leaving?'

'Of course, he will stay behind since you so desire it, but in that case you might as well give up your throne to him, you who tremble before the threats of a ten-year-old child. Give your seat up to him since you cannot rule. As for me, I am going to return to my parents' village for I will not be able to live under the tyranny of Sogolon's son. I will go and finish my days among my kinsfolk and I will say that I had a son who was afraid to rule.'

Sassouma bewailed her lot so much that Dankaran Touman suddenly revealed himself as a man of iron. Now he desired the death of his brothers—but he let them leave, it could not be helped, but if they should ever cross his path again——! He would reign, alone, for power could not be shared!

Thus Sogolon and her children tasted exile. We poor creatures! We think we are hurting our neighbour at the time when we are working in the very direction of destiny. Our action is not us for it is commanded of us.

Sassouma Bérété thought herself victorious because Sogolon and her children had fled from Mali. Their feet ploughed up the dust of the roads. They suffered the insults which those who leave their country know of. Doors were shut against them and kings chased them from their courts. But all that was part of the great destiny of Sundiata. Seven years passed, seven winters followed one another and forgetfulness crept into the souls of men, but time marched on at an even pace. Moons succeeded moons in the same sky and rivers in their beds continued their endless course.

Seven years passed and Sundiata grew up. His body became sturdy and his misfortunes made his mind wise. He became a man. Sogolon felt the weight of her years and of the growing hump on her back, while Djata, like a young tree, was shooting up to the sky.

After leaving Niani, Sogolon and her children had sojourned at

28

Djedeba with the king, Mansa Konkon, the great sorcerer. Djedeba was a town on the Niger two days away from Niani. The king received them with a little mistrust, but everywhere the stranger enjoys the right to hospitality, so Sogolon and her children were lodged in the very enclosure of the king and for two months Sundiata and Manding Bory joined in the games of the king's children. One night, as the children were playing at knuckle-bones outside the palace in the moonlight, the king's daughter, who was no more than twelve, said to Manding Bory, 'You know that my father is a great sorcerer.'

'Really?' said the artless Manding Bory.

'Why yes, you mean you did not know? Well anyway, his power lies in the game of wori;[34] you can play wori.'

'My brother now, he is a great sorcerer.'

'No doubt he does not come up to my father.'

'But what did you say? Your father plays at wori?'

Just then Sogolon called the children because the moon had just waned.

'Mother is calling us,' said Sundiata, who was standing at one side. 'Come Manding Bory. If I am not mistaken, you are fond of that daughter of Mansa Konkon's.'

'Yes brother, but I would have you know that to drive a cow into the stable it is necessary to take the calf in.'

'Of course, the cow will follow the kidnapper. But take care, for if the cow is in a rage so much the worse for the kidnapper.'

The two brothers went in swopping proverbs. Men's wisdom is contained in proverbs and when children wield proverbs it is a sign that they have profited from adult company. That morning Sundiata and Manding Bory did not leave the royal enclosure but played with the king's children beneath the meeting tree.[35] At the beginning of the afternoon Mansa Konkon ordered the son of Sogolon into his palace.

The king lived in a veritable maze and after several twists and turns through dark corridors a servant left Djata in a badly-lit room. He looked about him but was not afraid. Fear enters the heart of him who does not know his destiny, whereas Sundiata knew that he was striding towards a great destiny. He did not know what fear was. When his eyes were accustomed to the semi-darkness, Sundiata saw the king sitting with his back to the light on a great ox-hide. He saw some splendid weapons hanging on the walls and exclaimed:

'What beautiful weapons you have, Mansa Konkon,'[36] and, seizing a sword, he began to fence on his own against an imaginary foe. The king, astonished, watched the extraordinary child.

'You had me sent for,' said the latter, 'and here I am.' He hung the sword back up.

'Sit down,' said the king. 'It is a habit with me to invite my guests to play, so we are going to play, we are going to play at wori. But I make rather unusual conditions; if I win—and I shall win—I kill you.'

'And if it is I who win,' said Djata without being put out.

'In that case I will give you all that you ask of me. But I would have you know that I always win.'

'If I win I ask for nothing more than that sword,' said Sundiata, pointing to the sword he had brandished.

'All right,' said the king, 'you are sure of yourself, eh?' He drew up the log in which the wori holes were dug and put four pebbles in each of the holes.

'I go first,' said the king, and taking the four pebbles from one hole he dealt them out, punctuating his actions with these words:

> 'I don don, don don Kokodji.
> Wori is the invention of a hunter.
> I don don, don don Kokodji.
> I am unbeatable at this game.
> I am called the "exterminator king".'

And Sundiata, taking the pebbles from another hole, continued:

> 'I don don, don don Kokodji.
> Formerly guests were sacred.
> I don don, don don Kokodji.
> But the gold came only yesterday.
> Whereas I came before yesterday.'

'Someone has betrayed me,' roared the king Mansa Konkon, 'someone has betrayed me.'

'No, king, do not accuse anybody,' said the child.

'What then?'

'It is nearly three moons since I have been living with you and you have never up to now suggested a game of wori. God is the guest's tongue. My words express only the truth because I am your guest.'

The truth was that the queen mother of Niani had sent gold to Mansa Konkon so that he would get rid of Sundiata: 'the gold came only yesterday', and Sundiata was at the king's court prior to the gold. In fact, the king's daughter had revealed the secret to Manding Bory. Then the king, in confusion, said, 'You have won, but you will not have what you asked for, and I will turn you out of my town.'

'Thank you for two months' hospitality, but I will return, Mansa Konkon.'

Once again Sogolon and her children took to the path of exile. They went away from the river and headed west. They were going to seek hospitality from the king of Tabon in the country which is called the Fouta Djallon today. This region was at that time inhabited by the Kamara blacksmiths and the Djallonkés.[37] Tabon was an impregnable town firmly entrenched behind mountains, and the king had been for a long time an ally of the Niani court. His son, Fran Kamara, had been one of the companions of Sundiata. After Sogolon's departure from Niani the companion princes of Sundiata had been sent back to their respective families.

But the king of Tabon was already old and did not want to fall out with whoever ruled at Niani. He welcomed Sogolon with kindness and advised her to go away as far as possible. He suggested the court of Ghana,[38] whose king he knew. A caravan of merchants was shortly leaving for Ghana. The old king commended Sogolon and her children to the merchants and even delayed the departure for a few days to allow the mother to recover a little from her fatigues.

It was with joy that Sundiata and Manding Bory met Fran Kamara again. The latter, not without pride, showed them round the fortresses of Tabon and had them admire the huge iron gates and the king's arsenals. Fran Kamara was very glad to receive Sundiata at his home but was very grieved when the fatal day arrived, the day of departure. The night before he had given a hunting party to the princes of Mali and the youngsters had talked in the bush like men.

'When I go back to Mali,' Sundiata had said, 'I will pass

31

through Tabon to pick you up and we will go to Mali together.'

'Between now and then we will have grown up,' Manding Bory had added.

'I will have all the army of Tabon for my own,' Fran Kamara had said, 'The blacksmiths and the Djallonkés are excellent warriors. I already attend the gathering of armed men which my father holds once a year.'

'I will make you a great general, we will travel through many countries and emerge the strongest of all. Kings will tremble before us as a woman trembles before a man.' The son of Sogolon had spoken thus.

The exiles took to the road again. Tabon was very far from Ghana,[39] but the merchants were good to Sogolon and her children. The king had provided the mounts and the caravan headed to the north, leaving the land of Kita on the right. On the way the merchants told the princes a great deal about events of the past. Mari Djata was particularly interested in the stories bearing on the great king of the day, Soumaoro Kanté. It was to him at Sosso that Balla Fasséké had gone as envoy. Djata learnt that Saumaoro was the richest and most powerful king and even the king of Ghana paid him tribute. He was also a man of great cruelty.

The country of Ghana is a dry region where water is short. Formerly the Cissés of Ghana were the most powerful of princes. They were descended from Alexander the Great, the king of gold and silver, but ever since the Cissés had broken the ancestral taboo[40] their power had kept on declining. At the time of Sundiata the descendants of Alexander were paying tribute to the king of Sosso. After several days of travelling the caravan arrived outside Wagadou. The merchants showed Sogolon and her children the great forest of Wagadou, where the great serpent-god used to live.[41] The town was surrounded with enormous walls, very badly maintained. The travellers noticed that there were a lot of white traders at Wagadou[42] and many encampments were to be seen all around the town. Tethered camels were everywhere.

Ghana was the land of the Soninke,[43] and the people there did not speak Mandingo any more, but nevertheless there were many people who understood it, for the Soninke travel a lot. They are great traders. Their donkey caravans came heavily laden to

Niani every dry season. They would set themselves up behind the town and the inhabitants would come out to barter.

The merchants made their way towards the colossal city gate. The head of the caravan spoke to the guards and one of them beckoned to Sundiata and his family to follow him, and they entered the city of the Cissés. The terraced houses did not have straw roofs in complete contrast to the towns of Mali. There were also a lot of mosques in this city, but that did not astonish Sundiata in the least, for he knew that the Cissés were very religious;[44] at Niani there was only one mosque. The travellers noticed that the anterooms were incorporated in the houses whereas in Mali the anteroom or 'bollon' was a separate building. As it was evening everybody was making his way to the mosque. The travellers could understand nothing of the prattle which the passers-by exchanged when they saw them on their way to the palace.

The palace of the king of Ghana was an imposing building. The walls were very high and you would have thought it was a dwelling-place for jinn not for men. Sogolon and her children were received by the king's brother, who understood Mandingo. The king was at prayer, so his brother made them comfortable in an enormous room and water was brought for them to quench their thirst. After the prayer the king came back into his palace and received the strangers. His brother acted as interpreter.

'The king greets the strangers.'

'We greet the king of Ghana,' said Sogolon.

'The strangers have entered Wagadou in peace, may peace be upon them in our city.'

'So be it.'

'The king gives the strangers permission to speak.'

'We are from Mali,' began Sogolon. 'The father of my children was the king Naré Maghan, who, a few years ago sent a goodwill embassy to Ghana. My husband is dead but the council has not respected his wishes and my eldest son,' (she pointed to Sundiata) 'has been excluded from the throne. The son of my co-wife was preferred before him. I have known exile. The hate of my co-wife has hounded me out of every town and I have trudged along every road with my children. Today I have come to ask for asylum with the Cissés of Wagadou.'

There was silence for a few moments; during Sogolon's speech the king and his brother had not taken their eyes off Sundiata for an instant. Any other child of eleven would have been disconcerted by the eyes of adults, but Sundiata kept cool and calmly looked at the rich decorations of the king's reception hall—the rich carpets, the fine scimitars hanging on the wall—and the splendid garments of the courtiers.

To the great astonishment of Sogolon and her children the king also spoke in the very same Mandingo language.

'No stranger has ever found our hospitality wanting. My court is your court and my palace is yours. Make yourself at home. Consider that in coming from Niani to Wagadou you have done no more than change rooms. The friendship which unites Mali and Ghana goes back to a very distant age, as the elders and griots know. The people of Mali are our cousins.'

And, speaking to Sundiata, the king said in a familiar tone of voice, 'Approach, cousin, what is your name?'

'My name is Mari-Djata and I am also called Maghan, but most commonly people call me Sundiata. As for my brother, he is called Manding Boukary, my youngest sister is called Djamarou and the other Sogolon-Kolonkan.'

'There's one that will make a great king. He forgets nobody,'

Seeing that Sogolon was very tired, the king said, 'Brother, look after our guests. Let Sogolon and her children be royally treated and from tomorrow let the princes of Mali sit among our children.'

Sogolon recovered fairly quickly from her exertions. She was treated like a queen at the court of king Soumaba Cissé. The children were clothed in the same fashion as those of Wagadou. Sundiata and Manding Bory had long smocks splendidly embroidered. They were showered with so many attentions that Manding Bory was embarrassed by them, but Sundiata found it quite natural to be treated like this. Modesty is the portion of the average man, but superior men are ignorant of humility. Sundiata even became exacting, and the more exacting he became the more the servants trembled before him. He was held in high esteem by the king, who said to his brother one day, 'If he has a kingdom one day everything will obey him because he knows how to command.'

However, Sogolon found no more lasting peace at Wagadou than she had found at the courts of Djedeba or Tabon; she fell ill after a year.

34

King Soumaba Cissé decided to send Sogolon and her people to Mema to the court of his cousin, Tounkara. Mema was the capital of a great kingdom on the Niger beyond the land of Do. The king reassured Sogolon of the welcome she would be given there. Doubtless the air which blew from the river would be able to restore Sogolon's health.

The children were sorry to leave Wagadou for they had made many friends, but their destiny lay elsewhere and they had to go away.

King Soumaba Cissé entrusted the travellers to some merchants who were going to Mema. It was a large caravan and the journey was done by camel. The children had for a long time accustomed themselves to these animals which were unknown in Mali. The king had introduced Sogolon and her children as members of his family and they were thus treated with much consideration by the merchants. Always keen to learn, Sundiata asked the caravaneers many questions. They were very well-informed people and told Sundiata a lot of things. He was told about the countries beyond Ghana; the land of the Arabs; the Hejaz, cradle of Islam, and of Djata's ancestors (for Bibali Bounama, the faithful servant of the Prophet, came from Hejaz). He learnt many things about Alexander the Great, too, but it was with terror that the merchants spoke of Soumaoro, the sorcerer-king, the plunderer who would rob the merchants of everything when he was in a bad mood.

A courier, despatched earlier from Wagadou, had heralded the arrival of Sogolon at Mema; a great escort was sent to meet the travellers and a proper reception was held before Mema. Archers and spearmen formed up in a double line and the merchants showed even more respect to their travelling companions. Surprisingly enough, the king was absent. It was his sister who had organized this great reception. The whole of Mema was at the city gate and you would have thought it was the king's homecoming. Here many people could speak Mandingo and Sogolon and her children could understand the amazement of the people, who were saying to each other, 'Where do they come from? Who are they?'

The king's sister received Sogolon and her children in the palace. She spoke Maninkakan[45] very well and talked to Sogolon as if she had known her for a long time. She lodged Sogolon in a

35

wing of the palace. As usual, Sundiata very soon made his presence felt among the young princes of Mema and in a few days he knew every corner of the royal enclosure.

The air of Mema, the air of the river, did Sogolon's health a lot of good, but she was even more affected by the friendliness of the king's sister, who was called Massiran. Massiran disclosed to Sogolon that the king had no children and that the new companions of Sundiata were only the sons of Mema's vassal kings. The king had gone on a campaign against the mountain tribes who lived on the other side of the river. It was like this every year, because as soon as these tribes were left in peace they came down from the mountains to pillage the country.

Sundiata and Manding Bory again took up their favourite pastime, hunting, and went out with the young vassals of Mema.

At the approach of the rainy season the king's return was announced. The city of Mema gave a triumphal welcome to its king. Moussa Tounkara, richly dressed, was riding on a magnificent horse while his formidable cavalry made an impressive escort. The infantry marched in ranks carrying on their heads the booty taken from the enemy. The war drums rolled while the captives, heads lowered and hands tied behind their backs, moved forward mournfully to the accompaniment of the crowd's derisive laughter.

When the king was in his palace, Massiran, his sister, introduced Sogolon and her children and handed him the letter from the king of Ghana. Moussa Tounkara was very affable and said to Sogolon, 'My cousin Soumaba recommends you and that is enough. You are at home. Stay here as long as you wish.'

It was at the court of Mema that Sundiata and Manding Bory went on their first campaign. Moussa Tounkara was a great warrior and therefore he admired strength. When Sundiata was fifteen the king took him with him on campaign. Sundiata astonished the whole army with his strength and with his dash in the charge. In the course of a skirmish against the mountaineers he hurled himself on the enemy with such vehemence that the king feared for his life, but Mansa Tounkara admired bravery too much to stop the son of Sogolon. He followed him closely to protect him and he saw with rapture how the youth sowed panic among the enemy. He had remarkable presence of

36

mind, struck right and left and opened up for himself a glorious path. When the enemy had fled the old 'sofas'[46] said, 'There's one that'll make a good king.' Moussa Tounkara took the son of Sologon in his arms and said, 'It is destiny that has sent you to Mema. I will make a great warrior out of you.'

From that day Sundiata did not leave the king any more. He eclipsed all the young princes and was the friend of the whole army. They spoke about nothing but him in the camp. Men were even more surprised by the lucidity of his mind. In the camp he had an answer to everything and the most puzzling situations resolved themselves in his presence.

Soon it was in Mema itself that people began to talk about Sundiata. Was it not Providence which had sent this boy at a time when Mema had no heir? People already averred that Sundiata would extend his dominion from Mema to Mali. He went on all the campaigns. The enemy's incursions became rarer and rarer and the reputation of Sogolon's son spread beyond the river.

After three years the king appointed Sundiata Kan-Koro-Sigui, his Viceroy, and in the king's absence it was he who governed. Djata had now seen eighteen winters and at that time he was a tall young man with a fat neck and a powerful chest. Nobody else could bend his bow. Everyone bowed before him and he was greatly loved. Those who did not love him feared him and his voice carried authority.

The king's choice was approved of both by the army and the people; the people love all who assert themselves over them. The soothsayers of Mema revealed the extraordinary destiny of Djata. It was said that he was the successor of Alexander the Great and that he would be even greater; the soldiers already had a thousand dreams of conquest. What was impossible with such a gallant chief? Sundiata inspired confidence in the sofas by his example, for the sofa loves to see his chief share the hardship of battle.

Djata was now a man, for time had marched on since the exodus from Niani and his destiny was now to be fulfilled. Sogolon knew that the time had arrived and she had performed her task. She had nurtured the son for whom the world was waiting and she knew that now her mission was accomplished, while that of Djata was about to begin. One day she said to her son,

'Do not deceive yourself. Your destiny lies not here but in Mali. The moment has come. I have finished my task and it is yours that is going to begin, my son. But you must be able to wait. Everything in its own good time.'

Soumaoro Kanté, the Sorcerer King

While Sogolon's son was fighting his first campaign far from his native land, Mali had fallen under the domination of a new master, Soumaoro Kanté, king of Sosso.

When the embassy sent by Dankaran Touman arrived at Sosso, Suomaoro demanded that Mali should acknowledge itself tributary to Sosso. Balla Fasséké found delegates from several other kingdoms at Soumaoro's court. With his powerful army of smiths the king of Sosso had quickly imposed his power on everybody. After the defeat of Ghana and Diaghan[47] no one dared oppose him any more. Soumaoro was descended from the line of smiths called Diarisso who first harnessed fire and taught men how to work iron, but for a long time Sosso had remained a little village of no significance. The powerful king of Ghana was the master of the country. Little by little the kingdom of Sosso had grown at the expense of Ghana and now the Kantés dominated their old masters. Like all masters of fire, Soumaoro Kanté was a great sorcerer. His fetishes[48] had a terrible power and it was because of them that all kings trembled before him, for he could deal a swift death to whoever he pleased. He had fortified Sosso with a triple curtain wall and in the middle of the town loomed his palace, towering over the thatched huts of the villages.[49] He had had an immense seven-storey tower built for himself and he lived on the seventh floor in the midst of his fetishes. This is why he was called 'The Untouchable King'.

Soumaoro let the rest of the Mandingo embassy return but he kept Balla Fasséké back and threatened to destroy Niani if Dankaran Touman did not make his submission. Frightened, the son of Sassouma immediately made his submission, and he even sent his sister, Nana Triban, to the king of Sosso.

One day when the king was away, Balla Fasséké managed to

get right into the most secret chamber of the palace where Soumaoro safeguarded his fetishes. When he had pushed the door open he was transfixed with amazement at what he saw. The walls of the chamber were tapestried with human skins and there was one in the middle of the room on which the king sat; around an earthenware jar nine heads formed a circle; when Balla had opened the door the water had become disturbed and a monstrous snake had raised its head. Balla Fasséké, who was also well versed in sorcery, recited some formulas and everything in the room fell quiet, so he continued his inspection. He saw on a perch above the bed three owls which seemed to be asleep; on the far wall hung strangely-shaped weapons, curved swords and knives with three cutting edges. He looked at the skulls attentively and recognized the nine kings killed by Soumaoro. To the right of the door he discovered a great balafon, bigger than he had ever seen in Mali. Instinctively he pounced upon it and sat down to play. The griot always has a weakness for music, for music is the griot's soul.

He began to play. He had never heard such a melodious balafon. Though scarcely touched by the hammer, the resonant wood gave out sounds of an infinite sweetness, notes clear and as pure as gold dust; under the skilful hand of Balla the instrument had found its master. He played with all his soul and the whole room was filled with wonderment. The drowsy owls, eyes half closed, began to move their heads as though with satisfaction. Everything seemed to come to life upon the strains of this magic music. The nine skulls resumed their earthly forms and blinked at hearing the solemn 'Vulture Tune';[50] with its head resting on the rim, the snake seemed to listen from the jar. Balla Fasséké was pleased at the effect his music had had on the strange inhabitants of this ghoulish chamber, but he quite understood that this balafon was not at all like any other. It was that of a great sorcerer. Soumaoro was the only one to play this instrument. After each victory he would come and sing his own praises. No griot had ever touched it. Not all ears were made to hear that music. Soumaoro was constantly in touch with this xylophone and no matter how far away he was, one only had to touch it for him to know that someone had got into his secret chamber.

The king was not far from the town and he rushed back to his palace and climbed up to the seventh storey. Balla Fasséké heard hurried steps in the corridor and Soumaoro bounded into the room, sword in hand.

'Who is there?' he roared. 'It is you, Balla Fasséké!'

The king was foaming with anger and his eyes burnt fiercely like hot embers. Yet without losing his composure the son of Doua changed key and improvised a song in honour of the king:

> There he is, Soumaoro Kanté.
> All hail, you who sit on the skins of kings.
> All hail, Simbon of the deadly arrow.
> I salute you, you who wear clothes of human skin.

This improvised tune greatly pleased Soumaoro and he had never heard such fine words. Kings are only men, and whatever iron cannot achieve against them, words can. Kings, too, are susceptible to flattery, so Soumaoro's anger abated, his heart filled with joy as he listened attentively to this sweet music:

> All hail, you who wear clothes of human skin.
> I salute you, you who sit on the skins of kings.

Balla sang and his voice, which was beautiful, delighted the king of Sosso.

'How sweet it is to hear one's praises sung by someone else; Balla Fasséké, you will nevermore return to Mali for from today you are my griot.'

Thus Balla Fasséké, whom king Naré Maghan had given to his son Sundiata, was stolen from the latter by Dankaran Touman; now it was the king of Sosso, Soumaoro Kanté, who, in turn, stole the precious griot from the son of Sassouma Bérété. In this way war between Sundiata and Soumaoro became inevitable.

History

We are now coming to the great moments in the life of Sundiata. The exile will end and another sun will arise. It is the sun of Sundiata. Griots know the history of kings and kingdoms and that is why they are the best counsellors of kings. Every king wants to have a singer to perpetuate his memory, for it is the griot who rescues the memories of kings from oblivion, as men have short memories.

Kings have prescribed destinies just like men, and seers who probe the future know it. They have knowledge of the future, whereas we griots are depositories of the knowledge of the past. But whoever knows the history of a country can read its future.

Other peoples use writing to record the past, but this invention has killed the faculty of memory among them. They do not feel the past any more, for writing lacks the warmth of the human voice. With them everybody thinks he knows, whereas learning should be a secret.[51] The prophets did not write and their words have been all the more vivid as a result. What paltry learning is that which is congealed in dumb books!

I, Djeli Mamoudou Kouyaté, am the result of a long tradition. For generations we have passed on the history of kings from father to son. The narrative was passed on to me without alteration and I deliver it without alteration, for I received it free from all untruth.

Listen now to the story of Sundiata, the Na'Kamma, the man who had a mission to accomplish.

At the time when Sundiata was preparing to assert his claim over the kingdom of his fathers, Soumaoro was the king of kings, the most powerful king in all the lands of the setting sun. The fortified town of Sosso was the bulwark of fetishism against the word of Allah. For a long time Soumaoro defied the whole world. Since his accession to the throne of Sosso he had defeated nine kings whose heads served him as fetishes in his macabre chamber. Their skins served as seats and he cut his footwear from human skin. Soumaoro was not like other men, for the jinn had revealed themselves to him and his power was beyond measure. So his countless sofas were very brave since they believed their king to be invincible. But Soumaoro was an evil demon and his reign had produced nothing but bloodshed. Nothing was taboo for him. His greatest pleasure was publicly to flog venerable old men. He had defiled every family and everywhere in his vast empire there were villages populated by girls whom he had forcibly abducted from their families without marrying them.

The tree that the tempest will throw down does not see the storm building up on the horizon. Its proud head braves the winds even when it is near its end. Soumaoro had come to despise

41

everyone. Oh! how power can pervert a man. If man had but a mithkal[52] of divine power at his disposal the world would have been annihilated long ago. Soumaoro arrived at a point where he would stop at nothing. His chief general was his nephew the smith, Fakoli Koroma. He was the son of Soumaoro's sister, Kassia. Fakoli had a wonderful wife, Keleya, who was a great magician like her husband. She could cook better than the three hundred wives of Soumaoro put together.[53] Soumaoro adbucted Keleya and locked her up in his palace. Fakoli fell into a dreadful rage and went to his uncle and said, 'Since you are not ashamed to commit incest by taking my wife, I am freed from all my ties with you from this day forward. Henceforth I shall be on the side of your enemies. I shall combine insurgent Mandingoes with my own troops and wage war against you.' And he left Sosso with the smiths of the Koroma tribe.

It was like a signal. All those long-repressed hates and rancours burst out and everywhere men answered the call of Fakoli. Straight away Dankaran Touman, the king of Mali, mobilized and marched to join Fakoli. But Soumaoro, casting his nephew's threat aside, swooped down on Dankaran Touman, who gave up the struggle and fled to the land of the cola; and in those forested regions he founded the town of Kissidougou.[54] During this period Soumaoro, in his anger, punished all the Mandingo towns which had revolted. He destroyed the town of Niani and reduced it to ashes. The inhabitants cursed the king who had fled.

It is in the midst of calamity that man questions himself about his destiny. After the flight of Dankaran Touman, Soumaoro proclaimed himself king of Mali by right of conquest, but he was not recognized by the populace and resistance was organized in the bush. Soothsayers were consulted as to the fate of the country. The soothsayers were unanimous in saying that it would be the rightful heir to the throne who would save Mali. This heir was 'The Man with Two Names'. The elders of the court of Niani then remembered the son of Sogolon. The man with two names was no other than Maghan Sundiata.

But where could he be found? No one knew where Sogolon and her children lived. For seven years nobody had had any news of them. Now the problem was to find them. Nevertheless a search party was formed to seek him out. Among the people included must be mentioned Kountoun Manian, an old griot from the

42

court of Naré Maghan; Mandjan Bérété, a brother of Sassouma's, who did not want to follow Dankaran Touman in flight; Singhin Mara Cissé, a divine of the court; Siriman Touré, another divine; and, finally, a woman, Magnouma. According to the clues of the soothsayers they had to search towards the riverine lands, that is, towards the east. The searchers left Mali while war raged between Sosso Soumaoro and his nephew Fakoli Koroma.

The Baobab Leaves

At Mema Sundiata learnt that Soumaoro had invaded Mali and that his own brother, Dankaran Touman, had fled. He learnt also that Fakoli was holding his own against the king of Sosso. That year the kingdom of Mema was at peace and the king's viceroy had a lot of leisure time. As always, he went out hunting, but since the news about Mali had arrived Sundiata had become very gloomy. The aged Sogolon was ill. Manding Bory was fifteen and was now a lively youth like his brother and friend Sundiata. Djata's sisters had grown up and Kolonkan was now a tall maiden of marriageable age. Now that Sogolon had grown old it was she who did the cooking and she often went to the town market with her serving women.

Well, one day when she was at the market she noticed a woman who was offering for sale nafiola[55] and gnougou, condiments unknown to the people of Mema, who looked in astonishment at the woman who was selling them. Kolonkan approached. She recognized baobab leaves and many other vegetables which her mother used to grow in her garden at Niani.

'Baobab leaves,' she muttered, 'and gnougou, I know these,' she said, taking some.

'How do you know them princess?' said the woman. 'I have been offering them for sale here in the market of Mema for days but nobody wants any here.'

'But I am from Mali. At home my mother used to have a vegetable garden and my brother would go to seek baobab leaves for us.'

'What is your brother's name princess?'

'He is called Sogolon Djata, and the other one is called Manding Bory. I also have a sister called Sogolon Djamarou.'

Meanwhile a man had drawn near and he spoke thus to Sogolon Kolonkan, 'Princess, we are also from Mali. We are merchants and are going from town to town. I am selling colas myself. Here, I give you one. Princess, could your mother receive us today?'

'Of course, she will be happy to talk to people who come from Mali. Don't budge from here and I'll go and talk to her about it.'

Kolonkan, without caring about the scandal of the viceroy's sister being seen running across the market-place, had knotted her long dress about her middle and was running at full speed towards the royal enclosure.

'N'na,[56] she said, out of breath and addressing her mother, 'I have found baobab leaves, gnougou and many other things at the market, look. Some merchants from Mali are selling them. They would like to see you.'

Sogolon took the baobab leaves and gnougou in her hand and put her nose to them as though to inhale all the scent. She opened her eyes wide and looked at her daughter.

'They come from Mali, you say? Then run to the market and tell them that I am waiting for them, run, my daughter.'

Sogolon remained alone. She was turning the precious condiments over and over in her hands when she heard Sundiata and Manding Bory returning from the hunt.

'Hail, mother. We have returned,' said Manding Bory.

'Hail, mother,' said Sundiata, 'we have brought you some game.'

'Come in and sit down,' she said, and held out to them what she had in her hand.

'Why, it's gnougou,' said Sundiata, 'where did you find it? The people here grow it very little.'

'Yes, some merchants from Mali are offering it for sale in the market. Kolonkan has gone to fetch them for they want to see me. We are going to have some news of Mali.'

Kolonkan soon appeared followed by four men and a woman; straight away Sogolon recognized the eminent members of her husband's court. The salutations began and greetings were exchanged with all the refinement demanded by Mandingo courtesy. At last Sogolon said, 'Here are my children; they have

44

grown up far from their native country. Now let us talk of Mali.'

The travellers quickly exchanged meaningful glances, then Mandjan Bérété, Sassouma's brother, began to speak in these words:

'I give thanks to God the Almighty that we are here in the presence of Sogolon and her children. I give thanks to God that our journey will not have been in vain. It is two months since we left Mali. We went from one royal town to another posing as merchants and Magnouma offered vegetables of Mali for sale. In these eastern lands people are unacquainted with these vegetables. But at Mema our plan worked out perfectly. The person who bought some gnougou was able to tell us of your fate and that person, by a crowning stroke of fortune, turned out to be Sogolon Kolonkan.'

'Alas! I bring you sad tidings. That is my mission. Soumaoro Kanté, the powerful king of Sosso, has heaped death and desolation upon Mali. The king, Dankaran Touman, has fled and Mali is without a master, but the war is not finished yet. Courageous men have taken to the bush and are waging tireless war against the enemy. Fakoli Koroma, the nephew of the king of Sosso, is fighting pitilessly against his incestuous uncle who robbed him of his wife. We have consulted the jinn and they have replied that only the son of Sogolon can deliver Mali. Mali is saved because we have found you, Sundiata.'

'Maghan Sundiata, I salute you; king of Mali, the throne of your fathers awaits you. Whatever rank you may hold here, leave all these honours and come and deliver your fatherland. The brave await you, come and restore rightful authority to Mali. Weeping mothers pray only in your name, the assembled kings await you, for your name alone inspires confidence in them. Son of Sogolon, your hour has come, the words of the old Gnankouman Doua are about to come to pass, for you are the giant who will crush the giant Soumaoro.'

After these words a profound silence reigned over the room of Sogolon. She, her eyes cast down, remained silent; Kolonkan and Manding Bory had their eyes fixed on Sundiata.

'Very well,' he said, 'it is no longer the time for words. I am going to ask the king's leave and we will return immediately. Manding Bory, take charge of the envoys from Mali. The king

45

will return this evening and we will set out first thing tomorrow.'

Sundiata got up and all the envoys stood up while Djata went out. He was already king.

The king returned to Mema at nightfall. He had gone to spend the day in one of his neighbouring residences. The viceroy was not at the king's reception and nobody knew where he was. He returned at night and before going to bed he went and saw Sogolon. She had a fever and was trembling under the blankets. With a feeble voice she wished her son good night. When Sundiata was in his chamber alone he turned to the east and spoke thus:

'Almighty God, the time for action has come. If I must succeed in the reconquest of Mali, Almighty, grant that I may bury my mother in peace here.' Then he lay down.

In the morning, Sogolon Kedjou, the buffalo woman, passed away, and all the court of Mema went into mourning, for the viceroy's mother was dead. Sundiata went to see the king, who offered his condolences. He said to the king, 'King, you gave me hospitality at your court when I was without shelter. Under your orders I went on my first campaign. I shall never be able to thank you for so much kindness. However, my mother is dead; but I am now a man and I must return to Mali to claim the kingdom of my fathers. Oh king, I give you back the powers you conferred upon me, and I ask leave to depart. In any case, allow me to bury my mother before I go.'

These words displeased the king. Never did he think that the son of Sogolon could leave him. What was he going to seek in Mali? Did he not live happy and respected by all at Mema? Was he not already the heir to the throne of Mema? How ungrateful, thought the king, the son of another is always the son of another.

'Ungrateful creature,' said the king, 'since this is how it is, go away, leave my kingdom, but take your mother's remains with you; you will not bury her at Mema.'

But after a pause he went on, 'Very well then, since you insist on burying your mother, you will pay me the price of the earth where she will lie.'

'I will pay later,' replied Sundiata. 'I will pay when I reach Mali.'

'No, now, or you will have to take your mother's corpse with you.'

46

Then Sundiata got up and went out. He came back after a short while and brought the king a basket full of bits of pottery, guinea fowl feathers, feathers of young partridges and wisps of straw. He said, 'Very well king, here is the price of the land.'

'You are mocking, Sundiata, take your basket of rubbish away. That is not the price of the land. What do you mean by it?'

Then the old Arab who was the king's adviser said, 'Oh king, give this young man the land where his mother must rest. What he has brought you has a meaning. If you refuse him the land he will make war on you. These broken pots and wisps of straw indicate that he will destroy the town. It will only be recognized by the fragments of broken pots. He will make such a ruin of it that guinea-fowl and young partridges will come to take their dust baths there. Give him the land for if he reconquers his kingdom he will deal gently with you, your family, and his will be forever allied.'

The king understood. He gave him the land and Sogolon received her funeral honours with all the regal obsequies.

The Return

Every man to his own land! If it is foretold that your destiny should be fulfilled in such and such a land, men can do nothing against it. Mansa Tounkara could not keep Sundiata back because the destiny of Sogolon's son was bound up with that of Mali. Neither the jealousy of a cruel stepmother, nor her wickedness, could alter for a moment the course of great destiny.

The snake, man's enemy, is not long-lived, yet the serpent that lives hidden will surely die old. Djata was strong enough now to face his enemies. At the age of eighteen he had the stateliness of the lion and the strength of the buffalo. His voice carried authority, his eyes were live coals, his arm was iron, he was the husband of power.

Moussa Tounkara, king of Mema, gave Sundiata half of his army. The most valiant came forward of their own free will to follow Sundiata in the great adventure. The cavalry of Mema, which he had fashioned himself, formed his iron squadron.

Sundiata, dressed in the Muslim fashion of Mema, left the town at the head of his small but redoubtable army. The whole population sent their best wishes with him. He was surrounded by five messengers from Mali and Manding Bory rode proudly at the side of his brother. The horsemen of Mema formed behind Djata a bristling iron squadron. The troop took the direction of Wagadou, for Djata did not have enough troops to confront Soumaoro directly, and so the king of Mema advised him to go to Wagadou and take half of the men of the king, Soumaba Cissé. A swift messenger had been sent there and so the king of Wagadou came out in person to meet Sundiata and his troops. He gave Sundiata half of his cavalry and blessed the weapons. Then Manding Bory said to his brother, 'Djata, do you think yourself able to face Soumaoro now?'

'No matter how small a forest may be, you can always find there sufficient fibres to tie up a man. Numbers mean nothing; it is worth that counts. With my cavalry I shall clear myself a path to Mali.'

Djata gave out his orders. They would head south, skirting Soumaoro's kingdom. The first objective to be reached was Tabon, the iron-gated town in the midst of the mountains, for Sundiata had promised Fran Kamara that he would pass by Tabon before returning to Mali. He hoped to find that his childhood companion had become king. It was a forced march and during the halts the divines, Singbin Mara Cissé and Mandjan Bérété, related to Sundiata the history of Alexander the Great and several other heroes, but of all of them Sundiata preferred Alexander, the king of gold and silver, who crossed the world from west to east. He wanted to outdo his prototype both in the extent of his territory and the wealth of his treasury.

However, Soumaoro Kanté, being a great sorcerer, knew that the son of Sogolon had set out and that he was coming to lay claim to Mali. The soothsayers told him to forestall this calamity by attacking Sundiata, but good fortune makes men blind. Soumaoro was busy fighting Fakoli, the insurgent nephew who was holding out against him. Even before he had given battle the name of Sundiata was already well known throughout the kingdom. Those of the western frontier who had seen his army marching southwards spread extraordinary reports. Having just ascended the throne that year, Fran Kamara, the friend of Sundiata, had revolted in his turn against Soumaoro. In place of the policy of prudence followed by the old king of Tabon, Fran Kamara pursued a policy of war. Proud of his troops and above all spurred on by the imminent arrival of Sundiata, Fran Kamara, now called Tabon Wana (the Dread One of Tabon), had called to arms all the smiths and the mountain-dwelling Djallonkés.

Soumaoro sent a detachment under his son Sosso Balla to block Sundiata's route to Tabon. Sosso Balla was about the same age as Sundiata. He promptly deployed his troops at the entrance to the mountains to oppose Sundiata's advance to Tabon.

In the evening, after a long day's march, Sundiata arrived at the head of the great valley which led to Tabon. The valley was quite black with men, for Sosso Balla had deployed his men everywhere in the valley, and some were positioned on the heights which dominated the way through. When Djata saw the layout of Sosso Balla's men he turned to his generals laughing.

'Why are you laughing, brother, you can see that the road is blocked.'

'Yes, but no mere infantrymen can halt my course towards Mali,' replied Sundiata.

The troops stopped. All the war chiefs were of the opinion that they should wait until the next day to give battle because, they said, the men were tired.

'The battle will not last long,' said Sundiata, 'and the men will have time to rest. We must not allow Soumaoro the time to attack Tabon.'

Sundiata was immovable, so the orders were given and the war drums began to beat. On his proud horse Sundiata turned to right and left in front of his troops. He entrusted the rearguard, composed of a part of the Wagadou cavalry, to his younger brother Manding Bory. Having drawn his sword, Sundiata led the charge, shouting his war cry.

The Sossos were surprised by this sudden attack for they all thought that the battle would be joined the next day. The lightning that flashes across the sky is slower, the thunderbolts less frightening and floodwaters less surprising than Sundiata swooping down on Sosso Balla and his smiths. In a trice, Sundiata was in the middle of the Sossos like a lion in the sheepfold. The Sossos, trampled under the hooves of his fiery charger, cried out. When he turned to the right the smiths of Soumaoro fell in their tens, and when he turned to the left his sword made heads fall as when someone shakes a tree of ripe fruit. The horsemen of Mema wrought a frightful slaughter and their long lances pierced flesh like a knife sunk into a paw-paw. Charging ever forwards, Sundiata looked for Sosso Balla; he caught sight of him and like a lion bounded towards the son of Soumaoro, his sword held aloft. His arm came sweeping down but at that moment a Sosso warrior came between Djata and Sosso Balla and was sliced like a calabash. Sosso Balla did not wait and disappeared from amidst his smiths. Seeing their chief in flight, the Sossos gave way and fell into a terrible rout. Before the sun disappeared behind the mountains there were only Djata and his men left in the valley. Manding Bory, who was keeping an eye on the men perched on the heights, seeing that his brother had got the upper hand, dispatched some horsemen across the mountains to dislodge the Sossos. The Sossos were pursued until nightfall and several of them were taken prisoner.

Tabon Wana arrived too late, for the victory had already fallen to the son of Sogolon. The meeting of the two armies occasioned an all-night celebration in the very valley where the Sossos had been defeated. Tabon Wana Fran Kamara had a lot of food brought to the army of Sundiata and dancing went on all night, then at break of day the victors entered impregnable Tabon to the cheering of women standing on the ramparts.

The news of the battle of Tabon spread like wildfire in the plains of Mali. It was known that Soumaoro was not present at the battle, but the mere fact that his troops had retreated before Sundiata sufficed to give hope to all the peoples of Mali. Soumaoro realized that from now on he would have to reckon with this young man. He got to know of the prophecies of Mali, yet he was still too confident. When Sosso Balla returned with the remnant he had managed to save at Tabon, he said to his father, 'Father, he is worse than a lion; nothing can withstand him.'

'Be quiet, you ill-starred son,' Soumaoro had said, 'what, you tremble before a lad of your own age!' Nonetheless, these words of Balla made a deep impression on Soumaoro and he decided to march on Tabon with the largest of his forces.

The son of Sogolon had already decided on his plan of campaign—to beat Soumaoro, destroy Sosso and return triumphantly to Niani. He now had five army corps at his disposal, namely, the cavalry and infantry of Mema, those of Wagadou and the three tribes forming the army of Tabon Wana Fran Kamara. He must assume the offensive as soon as possible.

Soumaoro marched out to meet Sundiata. The meeting took place at Neguéboria in the Bouré country.[57] As usual, the son of Sogolon wanted to join battle straight away. Soumaoro thought to draw Sundiata into the plain, but Sundiata did not allow him the time to do it. Compelled to give battle, the king of Sosso drew up his men across the narrow valley of Neguéboria, the wings of his army occupying the slopes. Sundiata adopted a very original form of deployment. He formed a tight square with all his cavalry in the front line. The archers of Wagadou and Tabon were stationed at the back. Soumaoro was on one of the hills dominating the valley and he could be distinguished by his height and his helmet bristling with horns. Under an overpowering sun the trumpets sounded, on both sides the drums and bolons echoed and courage entered the hearts of the Sofas. Sundiata charged at the gallop and the valley soon disappeared in a cloud of red dust kicked up by thousands of feet and hooves. Without giving an inch, the smiths of Soumaoro stopped the wave.

As though detached from the battle, Soumaoro Kanté watched from the top of his hill. Sundiata and the king of Tabon were laying about them with mighty blows. Sundiata could be distinguished by his white turban and Soumaoro could see the breach he was opening up in the middle of his troops. The centre was about to cave in under the crushing pressure of Djata.

Soumaoro made a sign and from the hills came smiths swooping down into the bottom of the valley to encircle Sundiata. Then, without the slightest order from Sundiata, who was in the thick of the struggle, his square stretched and elongated itself into a great rectangle. Everything had been foreseen. The change was so quick that Soumaoro's men, halted in their mad career, could not use their weapons. In Djata's rear the archers of Wagadou and those of Tabon, on one knee, shot arrows into the sky, which fell thickly, like a rain of iron, on the ranks of Soumaoro. Like a stretching piece of elastic, Djata's line ascended to attack the hills. Djata caught sight of Sosso Balla and bore down on him, but the latter slipped away and the warriors of the buffalo woman's son raised a huzza of triumph. Soumaoro rushed up and his presence in the centre revived the courage of the Sossos. Sundiata caught sight of him and tried to cut a passage through to him. He struck to the right and struck to the left and trampled under-foot. The murderous hooves of his 'Daffeké'[58] dug into the chests of the Sossos. Soumaoro was now within spear range and Sundiata reared up his horse and hurled his weapon. It whistled away and bounced off Soumaoro's chest as off a rock and fell to the ground. Sogolon's son bent his bow but with a motion of the hand Soumaoro caught the arrow in flight and showed it to Sundiata as if to say 'Look, I am invulnerable.'

Furious, Sundiata snatched up his spear and with his head bent charged at Soumaoro, but as he raised his arm to strike his enemy he noticed that Soumaoro had disappeared. Manding Bory riding at his side pointed to the hill and said, 'Look, brother.'

Sundiata saw Soumaoro on the hill, sitting on his black-coated horse. How could he have done it, he who was only two paces from Sundiata? By what power had he spirited himself away on to the hill? The son of Sogolon stopped fighting to watch the king of Sosso. The sun was already very low and Soumaoro's smiths gave way but Sundiata did not give the order to pursue the enemy. Suddenly, Soumaoro disappeared!

How can I vanquish a man capable of disappearing and re-appearing where and when he likes? How can I affect a man in-vulnerable to iron? Such were the questions which Sogolon's son asked himself. He had been told many things about Sosso-Soumaoro but he had given little credence to so much gossip. Didn't people say that Soumaoro could assume sixty-nine differ-ent shapes to escape his enemies? According to some, he could transform himself into a fly in the middle of the battle and come and torment his opponent; he could melt into the wind when his enemies encircled him too closely—and many other things.

The battle of Neguéboria showed Djata, if he needed to be shown, that to beat the king of Sosso other weapons were necessary.

The evening of Neguéboria, Sundiata was master of the field, but he was in a gloomy mood. He went away from the field of battle with its agonized cries of the wounded, and Manding Bory and Tabon Wana watched him go. He headed for the hill where he had seen Soumaoro after his miraculous disappearance from

52

the midst of his troops. From the top of the hill he watched the compact mass of Soumaoro's smiths withdrawing in a cloud of dust.

'How was he able to escape me? Why did neither my spear nor my arrow wound him?' he wondered. 'What is the jinn that protects Soumaoro? What is the mystery of his power?'

His dismounted from his horse and picked up a piece of the earth which Soumaoro's horse had trampled on. Complete darkness had already fallen, the village of Neguéboria was not far away and the Djallonkés came out in a crowd to greet Sundiata and his men. The fires were already lit in the camp and the soldiers were beginning to prepare a meal, but what was their joy when they saw a long procession of girls from Neguéboria carrying on their heads enormous gourds of rice. All the sofas took up the girls' song in chorus. The chief of the village and its notables followed behind. Djata came down from the hill and received the Djallonké chief of Neguéboria, who was a vassal of Tabon Wana. For the sofas the day had been a victory because Soumaoro had fled, so the drums of war became drums of joy and Djata let his men celebrate what they called a victory. He stayed in his tent. In the life of every man there comes a moment when doubt settles in and the man questions himself on his own destiny, but on this evening it was not yet doubt which assailed Djata, for he was thinking rather of what powers he could employ to injure Sosso-Soumaoro. He did not sleep that night. At daybreak they struck camp. Peasants on their line of march told Sundiata that Soumaoro and his men were making a forced march without stopping so only in the evening did Sundiata halt the army to take a little food and rest. This was near the village of Kankigné. The men set up camp in the middle of the plain whilst guards were stationed on the heights. As usual, the men grouped themselves by tribes and busied themselves cooking their food. The tent of Sundiata stood in the middle of the camp surrounded by makeshift huts hastily built by the Mema horsemen.

But all of a sudden the sound of warning horns was heard. The men hardly had time to snatch their weapons before the camp was surrounded by enemies looming out of the darkness. The men of Mema were used to these surprise attacks on their camp and therefore unsaddled their horses. As the camp did not constitute a single unit, each kin group had to defend itself individually. Having escaped encirclement, Djata and the horsemen of Mema went to the help of Tabon Wana who seemed to be overwhelmed by numbers. In the pitch dark, no one knows how the men acquitted themselves. All that can be said is that the son of Sogolon broke the vice that was squeezing the breath out of Tabon Wana. The archers of Wagadou had quickly pulled themselves together and fired into the air torches and flaming arrows which fell among the enemy. Suddenly there was a panic. The burning brands crashed on to the bare backs of Soumaoro's sofas, cries of pain filled the sky and the Sossos began a headlong retreat while the cavalry cut them to pieces. The overwhelmed Sossos took to flight, again leaving many captives in the hands of Sundiata's men. Leaving to Tabon Wana the task of regrouping the men, Sundiata pursued the enemy with his cavalry to beyond the village of Kankigné. When he returned the struggle was over. The Sossos' night attack had caused more fright than real damage. On the ground near Tabon Wana's tent were found several split skulls. The king of Tabon never hit a man twice! The battle of Kankigné was not a great victory but it demoralized the Sossos. However, there had been great fear in Djata's ranks and that is why the griots sing:

'Kankigné Tabe bara djougonya.'[59]

The Names of the Heroes

The surprise attack at Kankigné had turned out badly for Soumaoro and succeeded only in increasing the wrath of Sundiata, who decimated the whole of the Sosso rearguard.

Soumaoro got back to Sosso to recover his strength while on all sides villages opened their gates to Sundiata. In all these villages Sundiata recruited soldiers. In the same way as light precedes the sun, so the glory of Sundiata, overleaping the mountains, shed itself on all the Niger plain.

All the rebellious kings of the savanna country had gathered at Sibi under the command of Kamandjan, the very same childhood friend of Sundiata and now himself the king of Sibi. Kamandjan and Tabon Wana were cousins, the former being the king of the Dalikimbon group of Kamaras, the latter being king of the iron-working Kamaras who were called Sinikimbon. Thus the Niani trio were going to meet again. Fakoli, the nephew of Soumaoro, had gone right to the south to recruit troops. He was bent on having his revenge on his uncle and recovering his wife, Keleya, she who was called 'the woman of the three hundred and thirty-three gourds of rice'.

Sundiata had now entered the region of the plains, the land of the powerful Niger. The trees that he saw were those of Mali, everything indicated that old Mali was near.

All the allies had arranged to meet up in the great plain of Sibi, and all the children of the savanna were there about their kings. There they were, the valorous sons of Mali, awaiting what destiny had promised them. Pennants[60] of all colours fluttered above the sofas divided up by tribes.

With whom should I begin; with whom end?

I shall begin with Siara Kouman Konaté. Siara Kouman Konaté, the cousin of Sundiata was there. He was the ancestor of those who live in the land of Toron. His spear-armed troops formed a thick hedge around him.

I will also mention Faony Kondé, Faony Diarra, the king of the land of Do whence came Sogolon. Thus the uncle had come to meet his nephew. Faony, king of Do and Kri, was surrounded by sofas armed with deadly arrows. They formed a solid wall around his standard.

You also will I cite, Mansa Traoré, king of the Traoré tribe; Mansa Traoré, the double-sighted king, was at Sibi. Mansa Traoré could see what was going on behind him just as other men can see in front of them. His sofas, formidable archers with quivers on their shoulders, thronged around him.

As for you, Kamandjan, I cannot forget you among those whom I extol, for you are the father of the Dalikimbon Kamaras. The Kamaras, armed with long spears, raised their menacing pikes around Kamandjan.

In short, all the sons of Mali were there, all those who say 'N'Ko',[61] all who speak the clear language of Mali were represented at Sibi.

When the son of the buffalo woman and his army appeared, the trumpets, drums and tam-tams blended with the voices of the griots. The son of Sogolon was surrounded by his swift horsemen and his horse pranced along. All eyes were fixed on the child of Mali, who shone with glory and splendour. When he was within call, Kamandjan made a gesture and the drums, tam-tams and voices fell silent. Leaving the ranks, the king of Sibi went towards Sundiata and cried, 'Maghan Sundiata, son of Sogolon, son of Naré Maghan, assembled Mali awaits you. Hail to you, I am Kamandjan, king of Sibi.'

Raising his hand, Maghan Sundiata spoke thus: 'I salute you all, sons of Mali, and I salute you, Kamandjan. I have come back, and as long as I breathe Mali will never be in thrall—rather death than slavery. We will live free because our ancestors lived free. I am going to avenge the indignity that Mali has under-gone.'

A shout of joy issuing from thousands of throats filled the whole heaven. The drums and tam-tams rumbled while the griots struck up Balla Fasséké's 'Hymn to the Bow'. It was thus that Sundiata met the sons of Mali gathered at Sibi.

Nana Triban and Balla Fasséké

Sundiata and his mighty army stopped at Sibi for a few days. The road into Mali lay open, but Soumaoro was not yet vanquished. The king of Sosso had mustered a powerful army and his sofas were numbered by the thousand. He had raised contingents in all the lands over which he held sway and got ready to pounce again on Mali.

With scrupulous care, Sundiata had made his preparations at Sibi. Now he had sufficient sofas to meet Soumaoro in the open field, but it was not a question of having a lot of troops. In order to defeat Soumaoro it was necessary first of all to destroy his magical power. At Sibi, Sundiata decided to consult the sooth-sayers, of whom the most famous in Mali were there.

On their advice Djata had to sacrifice a hundred white bulls, a hundred white rams and a hundred white cocks. It was in the middle of this slaughter that it was announced to Sundiata that his sister Nana Triban and Balla Fasséké, having been able to escape from Sosso, had now arrived. Then Sundiata said to Tabon

Wana, 'If my sister and Balla have been able to escape from Sosso, Soumaoro has lost the battle.'

Leaving the site of the sacrifices, Sundiata returned to Sibi and met his sister and his griot.

'Hail, my brother,' said Nana Triban.

'Greetings, sister.'

'Hail Sundiata,' said Balla Fasséké.

'Greetings, my griot.'

After numerous salutations, Sundiata asked the fugitives to relate how they had been able to elude the vigilance of a king such as Soumaoro. But Triban was weeping for joy. Since the time of their childhood she had shown much sympathy towards the crippled child that Sundiata had been. Never had she shared the hate of her mother, Sassouma Bérété.

'You know, Djata,' she said, weeping, 'for my part I did not want you to leave the country. It was my mother who did all that. Now Niani is destroyed, its inhabitants scattered, and there are many whom Soumaoro has carried off into captivity in Sosso.'

She cried worse than ever. Djata was sympathetic to all this, but he was in a hurry to know something about Sosso. Balla Fasséké understood and said, 'Triban, wipe away your tears and tell your story, speak to your brother. You know that he has never thought ill of you, and besides, all that was in his destiny.'

Nana Triban wiped her tears away and spoke.

'When you left Mali, my brother sent me by force to Sosso to be the wife of Soumaoro, whom he greatly feared. I wept a great deal at the beginning but when I saw that perhaps all was not lost I resigned myself for the time being. I was nice to Soumaoro and was the chosen one among his numerous wives. I had my chamber in the great tower where he himself lived. I knew how to flatter him and make him jealous. Soon I became his confidante and I pretended to hate you, to share the hate which my mother bore you. It was said that you would come back one day, but I swore to him that you would never have the presumption to claim a kingdom you had never possessed, and that you had left never to see Mali again. However, I was in constant touch with Balla Fasséké, each of us wanting to pierce the mystery of Soumaoro's magic power. One night I took the bull by the horns and said to Soumaoro: "Tell me, oh you whom kings mention with trembling, tell me Soumaoro, are you a man like others or

57

are you the same as the jinn who protects humans? No one can bear the glare of your eyes, your arm has the strength of ten arms. Tell me, king of kings, tell me what jinn protects you so that I can worship him also." These words filled him with pride and he himself boasted to me of the might of his Tana.[62] That very night he took me into his magic chamber and told me all.

'Then I redoubled my zeal to show myself faithful to his cause, I seemed more overwhelmed than him. It was even he who went to the extent of telling me to take courage, that nothing was yet lost. During all this time, in complicity with Balla Fasséké, I was preparing for the inevitable flight. Nobody watched over me any more in the royal enclosure, of which I knew the smallest twists and turns. And one night when Soumaoro was away, I left that fearsome tower. Balla Fasséké was waiting for me at the gate to which I had the key. It was thus, brother, that we left Sosso.'

Balla Fasséké took up the story.

'We hastened to you. The news of the victory of Tabon made me realize that the lion had burst his chains. Oh son of Sogolon, I am the word and you are the deed, now your destiny begins.'

Sundiata was very happy to recover his sister and his griot. He now had the singer who would perpetuate his memory by his words. There would not be any heroes if deeds were condemned to man's forgetfulness, for we ply our trade to excite the admiration of the living, and to evoke the veneration of those who are to come.

Djata was informed that Soumaoro was advancing along the river and was trying to block his route to Mali. The preparations were complete, but before leaving Sibi, Sundiata arranged a great military review in the camp so that Balla Fasséké, by his words, should strengthen the hearts of his sofas. In the middle of a great circle formed by the sofas, Balla Fasséké extolled the heroes of Mali. To the king of Tabon he said: 'You whose iron arm can split ten skulls at a time, you, Tabon Wana, king of the Sinikimbon and the Djallonké, can you show me what you are capable of before the great battle is joined?'

The griot's words made Fran Kamara leap up. Sword in hand and mounted on his swift steed he came and stood before Sundiata and said, 'Maghan Sundiata, I renew my oath to you in the sight of all the Mandingoes gathered together. I pledge myself to conquer or to die by your side. Mali will be free or the smiths of Tabon will be dead.'

The tribes of Tabon shouted their approval, brandishing their weapons, and Fran Kamara, stirred by the shouts of the sofas, spurred his charger and charged forward. The warriors opened their ranks and he bore down on a great mahogany tree. With one stroke of his sword he split the giant tree just as one splits a paw-paw. The flabbergasted army shouted, 'Wassa Wassa . . . Ayé . . .'[63]

Then, coming back to Sundiata, his sword held aloft, the king of Tabon said, 'Thus on the Niger plain will the smiths of Tabon cleave those of Sosso in twain.' And the hero came and fell in beside Sundiata.

Turning towards Kamandjan, the king of Sibi and cousin of the king of Tabon, Balla Fasséké said, 'Where are you, Kamandjan, where is Fama Djan?[64] Where is the king of the Dalikimbon Kamaras. Kamandjan of Sibi, I salute you. But what will I have to relate of you to future generations?'

Before Balla had finished speaking, the king of Sibi, shouting his war-cry, started his fiery charger off at full gallop. The sofas, stupefied, watched the extraordinary horseman head for the mountain that dominates Sibi. . . . Suddenly a tremendous din filled the sky, the earth trembled under the feet of the sofas and a cloud of red dust covered the mountain. Was this the end of the world? . . . But slowly the dust cleared and the sofas saw Kamandjan coming back holding a fragment of a sword. The mountain of Sibi, pierced through and through, disclosed a wide tunnel!

Admiration was at its highest pitch. The army stood speechless and the king of Sibi, without saying a word, came and fell in beside Sundiata.

Balla Fasséké mentioned all the chiefs by name and they all performed great feats; then the army, confident in its leadership, left Sibi.

Krina

Sundiata went and pitched camp at Dayala in the valley of the Niger. Now it was he who was blocking Soumaoro's road to the south. Up till that time, Sundiata and Soumaoro had fought each other without a declaration of war. One does not wage war without saying why it is being waged. Those fighting should make a declaration of their grievances to begin with. Just as a sorcerer ought not to attack someone without taking him to task for some evil deed, so a king should not wage war without saying why he is taking up arms.

Soumaoro advanced as far as Krina, near the village of Dayala on the Niger and decided to assert his rights before joining battle. Soumaoro knew that Sundiata also was a sorcerer, so, instead of sending an embassy, he committed his words to one of his owls. The night bird came and perched on the roof of Djata's tent and spoke. The son of Sogolon in his turn sent his owl to Soumaoro. Here is the dialogue of the sorcerer kings:

'Stop, young man. Henceforth I am the king of Mali. If you want peace, return to where you came from,' said Soumaoro.

'I am coming back, Soumaoro, to recapture my kingdom. If you want peace you will make amends to my allies and return to Sosso where you are the king.'

'I am king of Mali by force of arms. My rights have been established by conquest.'

'Then I will take Mali from you by force of arms and chase you from my kingdom.'

'Know, then, that I am the wild yam of the rocks; nothing will make me leave Mali.'

'Know, also that I have in my camp seven master smiths who will shatter the rocks. Then, yam, I will eat you.'

'I am the poisonous mushroom that makes the fearless vomit.'

'As for me, I am the ravenous cock, the poison does not matter to me.'

'Behave yourself, little boy, or you will burn your foot, for I am the red-hot cinder.'

'But me, I am the rain that extinguishes the cinder; I am the boisterous torrent that will carry you off.'

'I am the mighty silk-cotton tree that looks from on high on the tops of other trees.'

'And I, I am the strangling creeper that climbs to the top of the forest giant.'

'Enough of this argument. You shall not have Mali.'

'Know that there is not room for two kings on the same skin, Soumaoro; you will let me have your place.'

'Very well, since you want war I will wage war against you,

but I would have you know that I have killed nine kings whose heads adorn my room. What a pity, indeed, that your head should take its place beside those of your fellow madcaps.'

'Prepare yourself, Soumaoro, for it will be long before the calamity that is going to crash down upon you and yours comes to an end.'

Thus Sundiata and Soumaoro spoke together. After the war of mouths, swords had to decide the issue. Sogolon's son was in his tent when someone came to announce to him the arrival of Fakoli, Soumaoro's insurgent nephew. All the men stood to arms and the war chiefs drew up their men. When everything was in order in the camp, Djata and the Mandingo leaders received Fakoli followed by his warriors. Fakoli halted before Sundiata and spoke thus:

'I salute you, Sundiata. I am Fakoli Koroma, king of the tribe of Koroma smiths. Soumaoro is the brother of my mother Kassia. I have taken up arms against my uncle because he has outraged me. Without fearing incest he has pushed his effrontery to the lengths of robbing me of my wife Keleya. As for you, you are coming to reconquer the kingdom of your fathers, you are fighting Soumaoro. We have the same goal and therefore I come to place myself under your orders. I bring you my strong-armed smiths, I bring you sofas who do not know what fear is. Sundiata, I and my men are yours.'

Balla, Sundiata's griot, said, 'Fakoli, come and sit among your brothers whom Soumaoro's injustice has smitten, the judge folds you to his bosom. You could not do better than entrust your cause to the son of Sogolon.'

Sundiata made a sign indicating that the griot had spoken well, but he added, 'I defend the weak, I defend the innocent, Fakoli. You have suffered an injustice so I will render you justice, but I have my lieutenants about me and I would like to know their opinions.'

All the war chiefs agreed. Fakoli's cause became Sundiata's cause. Justice had to be granted to the man who came to implore justice. Thus Sundiata accepted Fakoli Da-Ba, Large-Mouthed Fakoli, among his war chiefs.

Sundiata wanted to have done with Soumaoro before the rainy season, so he struck camp and marched on Krina where Soumaoro was encamped. The latter realized that the decisive battle had come. Sundiata deployed his men on the little hill that dominates the plain. The great battle was for the next day.

In the evening, to raise the men's spirits, Djata gave a great feast, for he was anxious that his men should wake up happy in the morning. Several oxen were slaughtered and that evening Balla Fasséké, in front of the whole army, called to mind the history of old Mali. He praised Sundiata, seated amidst his lieutenants, in this manner:

'Now I address myself to you, Maghan Sundiata, I speak to you king of Mali, to whom dethroned monarchs flock. The time foretold to you by the jinn is now coming. Sundiata, kingdoms and empires are in the likeness of man; like him they are born, they grow and disappear. Each sovereign embodies one moment of that life. Formerly, the kings of Ghana extended their kingdom over all the lands inhabited by the black man, but the circle has closed and the Cissés of Wagadou are nothing more than petty princes in a desolate land. Today, another kingdom looms up, powerful, the kingdom of Sosso. Humbled kings have borne their tribute to Sosso, Soumaoro's arrogance knows no more bounds and his cruelty is equal to his ambition. But will Soumaoro dominate the world? Are we, the griots of Mali, condemned to pass on to future generations the humiliations which the king of Sosso cares to inflict on our country? No, you may be glad, children of the "Bright Country", for the kingship of Sosso is but the growth of yesterday, whereas that of Mali dates from the time of Bilali. Each kingdom has its childhood, but Soumaoro wants to force the pace, and so Sosso will collapse under him like a horse worn out beneath its rider.

'You, Maghan, you are Mali. It has had a long and difficult childhood like you. Sixteen kings have preceded you on the throne of Niani, sixteen kings have reigned with varying fortunes, but from being village chiefs the Keitas have become tribal chiefs and then kings. Sixteen generations have consolidated their power. You are the outgrowth of Mali just as the silk-cotton tree is the growth of the earth, born of deep and mighty roots. To face the tempest the tree must have long roots and gnarled branches. Maghan Sundiata, has not the tree grown?

'I would have you know, son of Sogolon, that there is not room for two kings around the same calabash of rice. When a new cock comes to the poultry run the old cock picks a quarrel with him and the docile hens wait to see if the new arrival asserts himself or yields. You have come to Mali. Very well, then, assert yourself. Strength makes a law of its own self and power allows no division. *That can only be one chief — no democracy.*

'But listen to what your ancestors did, so that you will know what you have to do.

'Bilali, the second of the name, conquered old Mali. Latal Kalabi conquered the country between the Niger and the Sankarani. By going to Mecca, Lahibatoul Kalabi, of illustrious memory, brought divine blessing upon Mali. Mamadi Kani made warriors out of hunters and bestowed armed strength upon Mali. His son Bamari Tagnokelin, the vindictive king, terrorized Mali with this army, but Maghan Kon Fatta, also called Naré Maghan, to whom you owe your being, made peace prevail and happy mothers yielded Mali a populous youth.

'You are the son of Naré Maghan, but you are also the son of your mother Sogolon, the buffalo-woman, before whom powerless sorcerers shrank in fear. You have the strength and majesty of the lion, you have the might of the buffalo.

'I have told you what future generations will learn about your ancestors, but what will we be able to relate to our sons so that your memory will stay alive, what will we have to teach our sons about you? What unprecedented exploits, what unheard-of feats? By what distinguished actions will our sons be brought to regret not having lived in the time of Sundiata?

'Griots are men of the spoken word, and by the spoken word we give life to the gestures of kings. But words are nothing but words; power lies in deeds. Be a man of action; do not answer me any more with your mouth, but tomorrow, on the plain of Krina, show me what you would have me recount to coming generations. Tomorrow allow me to sing the "Song of the Vultures" over the bodies of the thousands of Sossos whom your sword will have laid low before evening.'

It was on the eve of Krina. In this way Balla Fasséké reminded Sundiata of the history of Mali so that, in the morning, he would show himself worthy of his ancestors.

At break of day, Fakoli came and woke up Sundiata to tell him that Soumaoro had begun to move his sofas out of Krina. The son of Sogolon appeared dressed like a hunter king. He wore tight-fitting, ochre-coloured trousers. He gave the order to draw up the sofas across the plain, and while his chiefs bustled about, Manding Bory and Nana Triban came into Djata's tent.

'Brother,' said Manding Bory, 'have you got the bow ready?'

'Yes,' replied Sundiata. 'Look.'

He unhooked his bow from the wall, along with the deadly arrow. It was not an iron arrow at all, but was made of wood and pointed with the spur of a white cock. The cock's spur was the Tana of Soumaoro, the secret which Nana Triban had managed to draw out of the king of Sosso.

'Brother,' said Nana Triban, 'Soumaoro now knows that I have fled from Sosso. Try to get near him for he will avoid you the whole battle long.'

These words of Nana Triban left Djata worried, but Balla Fasséké, who had just come into the tent, said to Sundiata that the soothsayer had seen the end of Soumaoro in a dream.

The sun had risen on the other side of the river and already lit the whole plain. Sundiata's troops deployed from the edge of the river across the plain, but Soumaoro's army was so big that other sofas remaining in Krina had ascended the ramparts to see the battle. Soumaoro was already distinguishable in the distance by his tall headdress, and the wings of his enormous army brushed the river on one side and the hills on the other. As at Neguéboria, Sundiata did not deploy all his forces. The bowmen of Wagadou and the Djallonkés stood at the rear ready to spill out on the left towards the hills as the battle spread. Fakoli Koroma and Kamandjan were in the front line with Sundiata and his cavalry.

With his powerful voice Sundiata cried 'An gnewa.'[65] The order was repeated from tribe to tribe and the army started off. Soumaoro stood on the right with his cavalry.

Djata and his cavalry charged with great dash but they were stopped by the horsemen of Diaghan and a struggle to the death began. Tabon Wana and the archers of Wagadou stretched out their lines towards the hills and the battle spread over the entire plain, while an unrelenting sun climbed in the sky. The horses of Mema were extremely agile, and they reared forward with their fore hooves raised and swooped down on the horsemen of Diaghan, who rolled on the ground trampled under the horses' hooves. Presently the men of Diaghan gave ground and fell back towards the rear. The enemy centre was broken.

It was then that Manding Bory galloped up to announce to Sundiata that Soumaoro, having thrown in all his reserve, had swept down on Fakoli and his smiths. Obviously Soumaoro was bent on punishing his nephew. Already overwhelmed by the numbers, Fakoli's men were beginning to give ground. The battle was not yet won.

His eyes red with anger, Sundiata pulled his cavalry over to the left in the direction of the hills where Fakoli was valiantly enduring his uncle's blows. But wherever the son of the buffalo passed, death rejoiced. Sundiata's presence restored the balance momentarily, but Soumaoro's sofas were too numerous all the same. Sogolon's son looked for Soumaoro and caught sight of him in the middle of the fray. Sundiata struck out right and left and the Sossos scrambled out of his way. The king of Sosso, who did not want Sundiata to get near him, retreated far behind his men, but Sundiata followed him with his eyes. He stopped and bent his bow. The arrow flew and grazed Soumaoro on the shoulder. The cock's spur no more than scratched him, but the effect was immediate and Soumaoro felt his powers leave him. His eyes met Sundiata's. Now trembling like a man in the grip of a fever, the vanquished Soumaoro looked up towards the sun. A great black bird flew over above the fray and he understood. It was a bird of misfortune.

'The bird of Krina,' he muttered.

The king of Sosso let out a great cry and, turning his horse's head, he took to flight. The Sossos saw the king and fled in their turn. It was a rout. Death hovered over the great plain and blood poured out of a thousand wounds. Who can tell how many Sossos perished at Krina? The rout was complete and Sundiata then dashed off in pursuit of Soumaoro. The sun was at the middle of its course. Fakoli had caught up with Sundiata and they both rode in pursuit of the fugitives. Soumaoro had a good start. Leaving the plain, the king of Sosso had dashed across the open bush followed by his son Balla and a few Sosso chiefs. When night fell Sundiata and Fakoli stopped at a hamlet. There they took a little food and rest. None of the inhabitants had seen Soumaoro. Sundiata and Fakoli started off in pursuit again as soon as they were joined by some horsemen of Mema. They galloped all night and at daybreak Djata learnt from some peasants that some horsemen had passed that way when it was still dark. The king of Sosso shunned all centres of population for he knew that the inhabitants, seeing him on the run, would no longer hesitate to lay hands on him in order to get into favour with the new master. Soumaoro was followed by none but his son Balla. After having changed his mount at daybreak, the king of Sosso was still galloping to the north.

With difficulty Sundiata found the trail of the fugitives. Fakoli was as resolute as Djata and he knew this country better. It was difficult to tell which of these two men harboured the greatest hatred towards Soumaoro. The one was avenging his humiliated country while the other was prompted by the love of a wife. At noon the horses of Sundiata and Fakoli were out of breath and the pursuers halted at Bankoumana. They took a little food and Djata learnt that Soumaoro was heading for Koulikoro. He had only given himself enough time to change horses. Sundiata and Fakoli set off again straight away. Fakoli said, 'I know a short cut to Koulikoro, but it is a difficult track and our horses will be tired.'

'Come on,' said Djata.

They tackled a difficult path scooped out by the rain in a gully. Cutting across country they now crossed the bush until, pointing a finger in front of him, Fakoli said, 'Look at the hills over there which herald Koulikoro. We have made up some time.'

'Good,' replied Djata simply.

However, the horses were fatigued, they went more slowly and painfully lifted their hooves from the ground. As there was no village in sight, Djata and Fakoli dismounted to let their mounts get their wind back. Fakoli, who had a small bag of millet in his saddle, fed them. The two men rested under a tree. Fakoli even said that Soumaoro, who had taken an easy but lengthy route, would not arrive at Koulikoro until nightfall. He was speaking like a man who had ridden over the whole country.

They continued on their way and soon climbed the hills. Arrived at the top, they saw two horsemen at the bottom of the valley going towards the mountain.

'There they are,' cried Djata.

Evening was coming on and the sun's rays were already kissing the summit of Koulikoro mountain. When Soumaoro and his son saw the two riders behind them, they broke off and began to climb the mountain. The king of Sosso and his son Balla seemed to have fresher horses. Djata and Fakoli redoubled their efforts.

The fugitives were within spear range when Djata shouted to them, 'Stop, stop.'

Like Djata, Fakoli wanted to take Soumaoro alive. Keleya's husband sheered off and outflanked Soumaoro on the right, making his horse jump. He was going to lay hands on his uncle but the latter escaped him by a sudden turn. Through his impetus Fakoli bumped into Balla and they both rolled on the ground. Fakoli got up and seized his cousin while Sundiata, throwing his spear with all his might, brought Soumaoro's horse tumbling down. The old king got up and the foot race began. Soumaoro was a sturdy old man and he climbed the mountain with great agility. Djata did not want either to wound him or kill him. He wanted to take him alive.

The sun had just disappeared completely. For a second time the king of Sosso escaped from Djata. Having reached the summit of Koulikoro, Soumaoro hurried down the slope followed by Djata. To the right he saw the gaping cave of Koulikoro and without hesitation he entered the black cavern. Sundiata stopped in front of the cave. At this moment arrived Fakoli who had just tied the hands of Sosso Balla, his cousin.

'There,' said Sundiata, 'he has gone into the cave.'

'But it is connected to the river,' said Fakoli.

The noise of horses' hooves was heard and it turned out to be a detachment of Mema horsemen. Straight away the son of Sogolon sent some of them towards the river and had all the mountain guarded. The darkness was complete. Sundiata went into the village of Koulikoro and waited there for the rest of his army.[66]

The victory of Krina was dazzling. The remains of Soumaoro's army went to shut themselves up in Sosso. But the empire of Sosso was done for. From everywhere around kings sent their submission to Sundiata. The king of Guidimakhan sent a richly furnished embassy to Djata and at the same time gave his daughter in marriage to the victor. Embassies flocked to Koulikoro, but when Djata had been joined by all the army he marched on Sosso. Soumaoro's city, Sosso, the impregnable city, the city of smiths skilled in wielding the spear.

In the absence of the king and his son, Noumounkeba, a tribal chief, directed the defence of the city. He had quickly amassed all

67

that he could find in the way of provisions from the surrounding countryside.

Sosso was a magnificent city. In the open plain her triple rampart with awe-inspiring towers reached into the sky. The city comprised a hundred and eighty-eight fortresses and the palace of Soumaoro loomed above the whole city like a gigantic tower. Sosso had but one gate; colossal and made of iron, the work of the sons of fire. Noumounkeba hoped to tie Sundiata down outside of Sosso, for he had enough provisions to hold out for a year.

The sun was beginning to set when Sogolon-Djata appeared before Sosso the Magnificent. From the top of a hill, Djata and his general staff gazed upon the fearsome city of the sorcerer-king. The army encamped in the plain opposite the great gate of the city and fires were lit in the camp. Djata resolved to take Sosso in the course of a morning. He fed his men a double ration and the tam-tams beat all night to stir up the victors of Krina.

At daybreak the towers of the ramparts were black with sofas. Others were positioned on the ramparts themselves. They were the archers. The Mandingoes were masters in the art of storming a town. In the front line Sundiata placed the sofas of Mali, while those who held the ladders were in the second line protected by the shields of the spearmen. The main body of the army was to attack the city gate. When all was ready, Djata gave the order to attack. The drums resounded, the horns blared and like a tide the Mandingo front line moved off, giving mighty shouts. With their shields raised above their heads the Mandingoes advanced up to the foot of the wall, then the Sossos began to rain large stones down on the assailants. From the rear, the bowmen of Wagadou shot arrows at the ramparts. The attack spread and the town was assaulted at all points. Sundiata had a murderous reserve; they were the bowmen whom the king of the Bobos had sent shortly before Krina. The archers of Bobo are the best in the world. On one knee the archers fired flaming arrows over the ramparts. Within the walls the thatched huts took fire and the smoke swirled up. The ladders stood against the curtain wall and the first Mandingo sofas were already at the top. Seized by panic through seeing the town on fire, the Sossos hesitated a moment. The huge tower surmounting the gate surrendered, for Fakoli's smiths had made themselves masters of it. They got into the city where the screams of women and children brought the

68

Sossos' panic to a head. They opened the gates to the main body of the army.

Then began the massacre. Women and children in the midst of fleeing Sossos implored mercy of the victors. Djata and his cavalry were now in front of the awesome tower palace of Soumaoro. Noumounkeba, conscious that he was lost, came out to fight. With his sword held aloft he bore down on Djata, but the latter dodged him and, catching hold of the Sosso's braced arm, forced him to his knees whilst the sword dropped to the ground. He did not kill him but delivered him into the hands of Manding Bory.

Soumaoro's palace was now at Sundiata's mercy. While everywhere the Sossos were begging for quarter, Sundiata, preceded by Balla Fasséké, entered Soumaoro's tower. The griot knew every nook and cranny of the palace from his captivity and he led Sundiata to Soumaoro's magic chamber.

When Balla Fasséké opened the door to the room it was found to have changed its appearance since Soumaoro had been touched by the fatal arrow. The inmates of the chamber had lost their power. The snake in the pitcher was in the throes of death, the owls from the perch were flapping pitifully about on the ground. Everything was dying in the sorcerer's abode. It was all up with the power of Soumaoro. Sundiata had all Soumaoro's fetishes taken down and before the palace were gathered together all Soumaoro's wives, all princesses taken from their families by force. The prisoners, their hands tied behind their backs, were already herded together. Just as he had wished, Sundiata had taken Sosso in the course of a morning. When everything was outside of the town and all that there was to take had been taken out, Sundiata gave the order to complete its destruction. The last houses were set fire to and prisoners were employed in the razing of the walls. Thus, as Djata intended, Sosso was destroyed to its very foundations.

Yes, Sosso was razed to the ground. It has disappeared, the proud city of Soumaoro. A ghastly wilderness extends over the places where kings came and humbled themselves before the sorcerer king. All traces of the houses have vanished and of Soumaoro's seven-storey palace there remains nothing more. A field of desolation, Sosso is now a spot where guinea fowl and young partridges come to take their dust baths.

Many years have rolled by and many times the moon has traversed the heaven since these places lost their inhabitants. The bourein,[67] the tree of desolation, spreads out its thorny undergrowth and insolently grows in Soumaoro's capital. Sosso the Proud is nothing but a memory in the mouths of griots. The hyenas come to wail there at night, the hare and the hind come and feed on the site of the palace of Soumaoro, the king who wore robes of human skin.

Sosso vanished from the earth and it was Sundiata, the son of the buffalo, who gave these places over to solitude. After the destruction of Soumaoro's capital the world knew no other master but Sundiata.

The Empire

While Sosso succumbed to the mattocks of its own sons, Sundiata marched on Diaghan. The king of Diaghan had been Soumaoro's most formidable ally and after Krina he still remained faithful to Soumaoro's cause. He had shut himself up in his city, which was proud of its cavalry, but like a hurricane Sundiata beat upon Diaghan, the city of divines.[68] Like Sosso, Diaghan was taken in one morning. Sundiata had the heads of all the young men shaved and made sofas of them.

Sundiata had divided his army into three bodies; the first, under the command of Fakoli Koroma, waged war in Bambougou; the second, under the command of Fran Kamara, fought in the mountains of the Fouta; Sundiata and the main body of the army marched on the geat city of Kita.

Kita Mansa was a powerful king and was under the protection of the jinn of the great mountain which dominates the town of Kita, Kita Kourou. In the middle of the mountain was a little pool of magic water. Whoever got as far as this pool and drank its waters became powerful, but the jinn of the pool were very evil and only the king of Kita had access to the mysterious pool.

Sundiata camped to the east of Kita and demanded submission of the king. Vainglorious in the protection of the mountain jinn, Kita Mansa answered Djata with arrogance. Sogolon's son had in his army some infallible soothsayers. On their advice, Sundiata invoked the jinn of Kita Kourou and sacrificed to them a hundred white oxen, a hundred white rams and a hundred white cocks. All the cocks died on their backs, facing upwards; the jinn had replied favourably. Then Sundiata did not hesitate any longer and first thing in the morning he gave the signal to attack. The assaulting sofas sang the 'Hymn to the Bow'. Balla Fesséké, dressed as a great griot, rode at Djata's side. At the first assault the east gate surrendered, but there was no massacre at all. Men, women and children all were spared, but Kita Mansa had been killed outside his palace. Sundiata accorded him royal obsequies. Sundiata did not take one prisoner at Kita and the inhabitants, who were Kamaras, became his allies.

First thing next morning Sundiata determined to go into the mountain to sacrifice to the jinn and thank them for his victory over Kita. The whole army followed him. The mountain of Kita is as steep as a wall and Sundiata resolved to go all round it to receive the submission of the numerous villages lying at the foot of Kita Kourou. At Boudofou, a Kamara village, there was a great celebration between Kamandjan's tribes and the inhabitants. There was dancing and eating around the sacred stone of Bou-dofou. Today the Kamaras still sacrifice at this stone, but only those Kamaras who have known how to respect the Dio of their ancestors. In the evening the army camped at Kourou-Koto on the slope of the mountain opposite. Kita Djata was well received by the king Mansa Kourou and several tribes fraternized there.

At break of day Sundiata, followed by Balla Fasséké and a few members of the royal tribe of Mali,[69] went to the foot of a large rock. He sacrificed a hundred cocks to the jinn of the mountain, then, accompanied by Balla Fasséké alone, Sundiata went off in search of the pool. He found it in the midst of the mountain. He knelt down at the water's edge and said,

'Oh jinn of the water, Master of the Moghoya-Dji, master of the magic water, I sacrificed to you a hundred bulls, I sacrificed to you a hundred rams, and I sacrificed to you a hundred cocks. You gave me the victory but I have not destroyed Kita. I, the successor to Kita Mansa, come to drink the magic water, the moghoya dji.'

He scooped up some water in his two hands and drank. He found the water good and drank three times of it, then he washed his face.

When Djata rejoined his men his eyes had an unbearable brilliance. He radiated like a star. The moghoya dji had transfigured him.

From Kourou-Koto Sundiata returned to Kita, the trip round the mountain having lasted two days. At Kita he found delegations from the kingdoms conquered by Fakoli and Tabon Wana. The king of Mali stayed at Kita for some time and often went hunting with his brother Manding Bory and Sibi Kamandjan. The people of Kita never hunted the mountain game for fear of the jinn. As for Sundiata, he hunted on the mountain for he had become the chosen one of the jinn. A Simbon from his early years, he was well enough versed in the art of Sané ni Kondolon. He and his companions used to bathe in one of the mountain springs and the people of Kita still distinguish this spring and surround it with great veneration.[70]

Leaving Kita, Sundiata and his large army headed for Do, the country of his mother Sogolon. At Do Sundiata was received as the uncle receives the nephew. Djata and Balla Fasséké betook themselves to the famous plain of Ourantamba and a member of the Traoré tribe accompanied them. The inhabitants of Do had raised a great mound on the spot where the buffalo had expired. Sundiata sacrificed a white cock on the mound. When the cock had died on its back a big whirlwind swirled up and blew towards the west.

'Look,' said Balla Fasséké, 'the whirlwind is going towards Mali.'

'Yes, it is time to go back there.'

From Do, Sundiata sent a richly furnished embassy to Mema loaded with costly gifts. Thus he paid off his contracted debt and the embassy made it known to the king that the Cissé-Tounkaras and the Keitas would be allies for ever.

It was from Do, also, that Sundiata ordered all his generals to meet him at Ka-ba on the Niger in the land of the king of Sibi. Fakoli had completed his conquests and the king of Tabon had subjugated the mountaineers of the Fouta. The arms of Sundiata had subdued all the countries of the savanna. From Ghana in the north to Mali in the south and from Mema in the east to the Fouta in the west, all the lands had recognized Sundiata's authority.

Djata's army followed the Niger valley to make its way to Ka-ba.

Kouroukan Fougan or
The Division of the World

Leaving Do, the land of ten thousand guns, Sundiata wended his way to Ka-ba, keeping to the river valley. All his armies converged on Ka-ba and Fakoli and Tabon Wana entered it laden with booty. Sibi Kamandjan had gone ahead of Sundiata to prepare the great assembly which was to gather at Ka-ba, a town situated on the territory belonging to the country of Sibi.

Ka-ba was a small town founded by Niagalin M'Bali Faly, a hunter of Sibi, and by Sounoumba Traore, a fisherman. Ka-ba belonged to the king of Sibi and nowadays you can also find Keitas at Ka-ba, but the Keitas did not come there until after Sundiata's time.[71] Ka-ba stands on the left bank of the Niger and it is through Ka-ba that the road to old Mali passes.

To the north of the town stretches a spacious clearing and it is there that the great assembly was to foregather. King Kamandjan had the whole clearing cleaned up and a great dais was got ready. Even before Djata's arrival the delegations from all the conquered peoples had made their way to Ka-ba. Huts were hastily built to house all these people. When all the armies had reunited, camps had to be set up in the big plain lying between the river and the town. On the appointed day the troops were drawn up on the vast square that had been prepared. As at Sibi, each people was gathered round its king's pennant. Sundiata had put on robes such as are worn by a great Muslim king.[72] Balla Fasséké, the high master of ceremonies, set the allies around Djata's great throne. Everything was in position. The sofas, forming a vast semicircle bristling with spears, stood motionless. The delegations of the various peoples had been planted at the foot of the dais. A complete silence reigned. On Sundiata's right, Balla Fasséké, holding his mighty spear, addressed the throng in this manner:

'Peace reigns today in the whole country; may it always be thus. . . .'

'Amen,' replied the crowd, then the herald continued:

'I speak to you, assembled peoples. To those of Mali I convey Maghan Sundiata's greeting; greetings to those of Do, greetings to those of Ghana, to those from Mema greetings, and to those of Fakoli's tribe. Greetings to the Bobo warriors and, finally, greetings to those of Sibi and Ka-ba. To all the peoples assembled, Djata gives greetings.

'May I be humbly forgiven if I have made any omission. I am nervous before so many people gathered together.

'Peoples, here we are, after years of hard trials, gathered around our saviour, the restorer of peace and order. From the east to the west, from the north to the south, everywhere his victorious arms have established peace. I convey to you the greetings of Soumaoro's vanquisher, Maghan Sundiata, king of Mali.

'But in order to respect tradition, I must first of all address myself to the host of us all, Kamandjan, king of Sibi; Djata greets you and gives you the floor.'

Kamandjan, who was sitting close by Sundiata, stood up and stepped down from the dais. He mounted his horse and brandished his sword, crying 'I salute you all, warriors of Mali, of Do, of Tabon, of Mema, of Wagadou, of Bobo, of Fakoli . . .; warriors, peace has returned to our homes, may God long preserve it.'

'Amen,' replied the warriors and the crowd. The king of Sibi continued.

'In the world man suffers for a season, but never eternally. Here we are at the end of our trials. We are at peace. May God be praised. But we owe this peace to one man who, by his courage and his valiance, was able to lead our troops to victory.

'Which one of us, alone, would have dared face Soumaoro? Ay, we were all cowards. How many times did we pay him tribute? The insolent rogue thought that everything was permitted him. What family was not dishonoured by Soumaoro? He took our daughters and wives from us and we were more craven than women. He carried his insolence to the point of stealing the wife of his nephew Fakoli! We were prostrated and humiliated in front of our children. But it was in the midst of so many calamities that our destiny suddenly changed. A new sun arose in the east. After the battle of Tabon we felt ourselves to be men, we realized that Soumaoro was a human being and not an incarnation of the devil, for he was no longer invincible. A man came to us. He had heard our groans and came to our aid, like a father when he sees his son in tears. Here is that man. Maghan Sundiata, the man with two names foretold by the soothsayers.

'It is to you that I now address myself, son of Sogolon, you, the nephew of the valorous warriors of Do. Henceforth it is from you that I derive my kingdom for I acknowledge you my sovereign. My tribe and I place ourselves in your hands. I salute you, supreme chief, I salute you, Fama of Famas.[73] I salute you, Mansa!'[74]

The huzza that greeted these words was so loud that you could hear the echo repeat the tremendous clamour twelve times over. With a strong hand Kamandjan stuck his spear in the ground in front of the dais and said, 'Sundiata, here is my spear, it is yours.'

Then he climbed up to sit in his place. Thereafter, one by one, the twelve kings of the bright savanna country got up and proclaimed Sundiata 'Mansa' in their turn. Twelve royal spears were stuck in the ground in front of the dais. Sundiata had become emperor. The old tabala of Niani announced to the world that the lands of the savanna had provided themselves with one single king. When the imperial tabala had stopped reverberating, Balla Fasséké, the grand master of ceremonies, took the floor again following the crowd's ovation.

'Sundiata, Maghan Sundiata, king of Mali, in the name of the twelve kings of the "Bright Country", I salute you as "Mansa".'

The crowd shouted 'Wassa, Wassa. . . . Ayé.'

It was amid such joy that Balla Fasséké composed the great hymn 'Niama' which the griots still sing:

> Niama, Niama, Niama,
> You, you serve as a shelter for all,
> All come to seek refuge under you.
> And as for you, Niama,
> Nothing serves you for shelter,
> God alone protects you.[75]

The festival began. The musicians of all the countries were there. Each people in turn came forward to the dais under Sundiata's impassive gaze. Then the war dances began. The sofas of all the countries had lined themselves up in six ranks amid a great clatter of bows and spears knocking together. The war chiefs were on horseback. The warriors faced the enormous dais and at a signal from Balla Fasséké, the musicians, massed on the right of the dais, struck up. The heavy war drums thundered, the bolons gave off muted notes while the griot's voice gave the throng the pitch for the 'Hymn to the Bow'. The spearmen, advancing like hyenas in the night, held their spears above their heads; the archers of Wagadou and Tabon, walking with a noiseless tread, seemed to be lying in ambush behind bushes. They rose suddenly to their feet and let fly their arrows at imaginary enemies. In front of the great dais the Kéké-Tigui, or war chiefs, made their horses perform dance steps under the eyes of the Mansa. The horses whinnied and reared, then, overmasteréd by the spurs, knelt, got up and cut little capers, or else scraped the ground with their hooves.

The rapturous people shouted the 'Hymn to the Bow' and clapped their hands. The sweating bodies of the warriors glistened in the sun while the exhausting rhythm of the tam-tams wrenched from them shrill cries. But presently they made way for the cavalry, beloved by Djata. The horsemen of Mema threw their swords in the air and caught them in flight, uttering mighty shouts. A smile of contentment took shape on Sundiata's lips, for he was happy to see his cavalry manoeuvre with so much skill.

In the afternoon the festivity took on a new aspect. It began with the procession of prisoners and booty. Their hands tied behind their backs and in triple file, the Sosso prisoners made their entry into the giant circle. All their heads had been shaved. Inside the circle they turned and passed by the foot of the dais. Their eyes lowered, the poor prisoners walked in silence, abuse heaped upon them by the frenzied crowd. Behind came the kings who had remained faithful to Soumaoro and who had not intended to make their submission. They also had their heads shorn, but they were on horseback so that everyone could see them. At last, right at the back, came Sosso Balla, who had been placed in the midst of his father's fetishes. The fetishes had been loaded onto donkeys. The crowd gave loud cries of horror on seeing the inmates of Soumaoro's grisly chamber. People pointed with terror at the snake's pitcher, the magic balafon, and the king of Sosso's owls. Soumaoro's son Balla, his hands bound, was on a horse but did not dare look up at this throne, which formerly used to tremble with fear at mere talk of his father. In the crowd could be heard:

'Each in his turn, Sosso Balla; lift up your head a bit, impudent little creature!' Or else: 'Did you have any idea that one day you would be a slave, you vile fellow!'

'Look at your useless fetishes. Call on them then, son of a sorcerer!'

When Sosso Balla was in front of the dais, Djata made a gesture. He had just remembered the mysterious disappearance of Soumaoro inside the mountain. He became morose, but his griot Balla Fasséké noticed it and so he spoke thus:

'The son will pay for the father, Soumaoro can thank God that he is already dead.'

When the procession had finished Balla Fasséké silenced everyone. The sofas got into line and the tam-tams stopped.

Sundiata got up and a graveyard silence settled on the whole place. The Mansa moved forward to the edge of the dais. Then Sundiata spoke as Mansa. Only Balla Fasséké could hear him, for a Mansa does not speak like a town-crier.

'I greet all the peoples gathered here.' And Djata mentioned them all. Pulling the spear of Kamandjan, king of Sibi, out of the ground, he said:

'I give you back your kingdom, king of Sibi, for you have deserved it by your bravery; I have known you since childhood and your speech is as frank as your heart is straightforward.

'Today I ratify for ever the alliance between the Kamaras of Sibi and the Keitas of Mali. May these two people be brothers henceforth. In future, the land of the Keitas shall be the land of the Kamaras, and the property of the Kamaras shall be henceforth the property of the Keitas.

'May there nevermore be falsehood between a Kamara and a Keita, and may the Kamaras feel at home in the whole extent of my empire.'

He returned the spear to Kamandjan and the king of Sibi prostrated himself before Djata, as is done when honoured by a Fama.

Sundiata took Tabon Wana's spear and said, 'Fran Kamara, my friend, I return your kingdom to you. May the Djallonkés and Mandingoes be forever allies. You received me in your own domain, so may the Djallonkés be received as friends throughout Mali. I leave you the lands you have conquered, and henceforth your children and your children's children will grow up at the court of Niani where they will be treated like the princes of Mali.'

One by one all the kings received their kingdoms from the very hands of Sundiata, and each one bowed before him as one bows before a Mansa.

Sundiata pronounced all the prohibitions which still obtain in relations between the tribes. To each he assigned its land, he established the rights of each people and ratified their friendships. The Kondés of the land of Do became henceforth the uncles of the imperial family of Keita, for the latter, in memory of the fruitful marriage between Naré Maghan and Sogolon, had to take a wife in Do. The Tounkaras and the Cissés became 'banter-brothers' of the Keitas. While the Cissés, Bérétés and Tourés were proclaimed great divines of the empire. No kin group was forgotten at Kouroukan Fougan; each had its share in the division. To Fakoli Koroma, Sundiata gave the kingdom of Sosso, the majority of whose inhabitants were enslaved. Fakoli's tribe, the Koromas, which others call Doumbouya or Sissoko, had the monopoly of the forge, that is, of iron working. Fakoli also received from Sundiata part of the lands situated between the Bafing and Bagbé rivers. Wagadou and Mema kept their kings who continued to bear the title of Mansa, but these two kingdoms acknowledged the suzerainty of the supreme Mansa. The Konaté of Toron became the cadets of the Keitas so that on reaching maturity a Konaté could call himself Keita.

When Sogolon's son had finished distributing lands and power he turned to Balla Fasséké, his griot, and said: 'As for you, Balla Fasséké, my griot, I make you grand master of ceremonies. Henceforth the Keitas will choose their griot from your tribe, from among the Kouyatés. I give the Kouyatés the right to make jokes about all the tribes, and in particular about the royal tribe of Keita.'

Thus spoke the son of Sogolon at Kouroukan Fougan. Since that time his respected word has become law, the rule of conduct for all the peoples who were represented at Ka-ba.

So, Sundiata had divided the world at Kouroukan Fougan. He kept for his tribe the blessed country of Kita, but the Kamaras inhabiting the region remained masters of the soil.

If you go to Ka-ba, go and see the glade of Kouroukan Fougan and you will see a linké tree planted there, perpetuating the memory of the great gathering which witnessed the division of the world.

Niani

After this great assembly Sundiata stayed a few more days at Ka-ba. For the people these were days of festivity. For them Djata caused hundreds of oxen, taken from Soumaoro's immense exchequer, to be slaughtered every day. In the main square of Ka-ba the girls of the town came and laid big calabashes of rice and meat at the foot of the observation platforms. Anybody could come and eat his fill and go away. Soon Ka-ba was full of people who had come from all directions attracted by the opulence. A year of war had emptied all the granaries so each came to take his share of the king of Sosso's reserves. It is even said that certain people had set up their household gods on that very spot during Djata's stay at Ka-ba. These were the summer months so these people slept on the observation platforms during the night and on awakening found calabashes of rice at their feet. That was the time when people sang the 'Hymn to Abundance' in Sundiata's honour:

> He has come
> And happiness has come
> Sundiata is here
> And happiness is here.

But it was time to return to his native Mali. Sundiata assembled his army in the plain and each people provided a contingent to accompany the Mansa to Niani. At Ka-ba all the peoples separated in friendship and in joy at their new-found peace.

Sundiata and his men had to cross the Niger in order to enter old Mali. One might have thought that all the dug-out canoes in the world had arranged to meet at the port of Ka-ba. It was the dry season and there was not much water in the river. The fishing tribe of Somono, to whom Djata had given the monopoly of the water, were bent on expressing their thanks to the son of Sogolon. They put all their dug-outs side by side across the Niger so that Sundiata's sofas could cross without wetting their feet.

When the whole army was on the other side of the river, Sundiata ordered great sacrifices. A hundred oxen and a hundred rams were sacrificed. It was thus that Sundiata thanked God on returning to Mali.

The villages of Mali gave Maghan Sundiata an unprecedented welcome. At normal times a traveller on foot can cover the distance from Ka-ba to Niani with only two halts, but Sogolon's son with his army took three days. The road to Mali from the river was flanked by a double human hedge. Flocking from every corner of Mali, all the inhabitants were resolved to see their saviour from close up. The women of Mali tried to create a sensation and they did not fail. At the entrance to each village they had carpeted the road with their multi-coloured pagnes so that Sundiata's horse would not so much as dirty its feet on entering their village. At the village exits the children, holding leafy branches in their hands, greeted Djata with cries of 'Wassa, Wassa, Ayé'.

Sundiata was leading the van. He had donned his costume of a hunter king—a plain smock, skin-tight trousers and his bow slung across his back. At his side Balla Fasséké was still wearing his festive garments gleaming with gold. Between Djata's general staff and the army Sosso Balla had been placed, amid his father's fetishes. But his hands were no longer tied. As at Ka-ba, abuse was everywhere heaped upon him and the prisoner did not dare look up at the hostile crowd. Some people, always ready to feel sympathy, were saying among themselves:

'How few things good fortune prizes!'

'Yes, the day you are fortunate is also the day when you are the most unfortunate, for in good fortune you cannot imagine what suffering is.'

The troops were marching along singing the 'Hymn to the Bow', which the crowd took up. New songs flew from mouth to mouth. Young women offered the soldiers cool water and cola nuts. And so the triumphal march across Mali ended outside Niani, Sundiata's city.

It was a ruined town which was beginning to be rebuilt by its inhabitants. A part of the ramparts had been destroyed and the charred walls still bore the marks of the fire. From the top of the hill Djata looked on Niani, which looked like a dead city. He saw the plain of Sounkarani, and he also saw the site of the young baobab tree. The survivors of the catastrophe were standing in rows on the Mali road. The children were waving branches, a few young women were singing, but the adults were mute.

'Rejoice,' said Balla Fasséké to Sundiata, 'for your part you will have the bliss of rebuilding Niani, the city of your fathers, but nevermore will anyone rebuild Sosso out of its ruins. Men will lose recollection of the very site of Soumaoro's city.'

With Sundiata peace and happiness entered Niani. Lovingly Sogolon's son had his native city rebuilt. He restored in the ancient style his father's old enclosure where he had grown up. People came from all the villages of Mali to settle in Niani. The walls had to be destroyed to enlarge the town, and new quarters were built for each kin group in the enormous army.

Sundiata had left his brother Manding Bory at Bagadou-Djeliba on the river. He was Sundiata's Kankoro Sigui, that is to say, viceroy. Manding Bory had looked after all the conquered countries. When reconstruction of the capital was finished he went to wage war in the south in order to frighten the forest peoples. He received an embassy from the country of Sangaran where a few Kondé clans had settled, and although these latter had not been represented at Kouroukan Fougan, Sundiata granted his alliance and they were placed on the same footing as the Kondés of the land of Do.

After a year Sundiata held a new assembly at Niani, but this one was the assembly of dignitaries and kings of the empire. The kings and notables of all the tribes came to Niani. The kings spoke of their administration and the dignitaries talked of their kings. Fakoli, the nephew of Soumaoro, having proved himself too independent, had to flee to evade the Mansa's anger. His lands were confiscated and the taxes of Sosso were payed directly into the granaries of Niani. In this way, every year, Sundiata gathered about him all the kings and notables; so justice prevailed everywhere, for the kings were afraid of being denounced at Niani.

Djata's justice spared nobody. He followed the very word of God. He protected the weak against the strong and people would make journeys lasting several days to come and demand justice of him. Under his sun the upright man was rewarded and the wicked one punished.

In their new-found peace the villages knew prosperity again, for with Sundiata happiness had come into everyone's home. Vast fields of millet, rice, cotton, indigo and fonio surrounded the villages. Whoever worked always had something to live on. Each year long caravans carried the taxes in kind[75] to Niani.

You could go from village to village without fearing brigands. A thief would have his right hand chopped off and if he stole again he would be put to the sword.

New villages and new towns sprang up in Mali and elsewhere. 'Dyulas', or traders, became numerous and during the reign of Sundiata the world knew happiness.

There are some kings who are powerful through their military strength. Everybody trembles before them, but when they die nothing but ill is spoken of them. Others do neither good nor ill and when they die they are forgotten. Others are feared because they have power, but they know how to use it and they are loved because they love justice. Sundiata belonged to this group. He was feared, but loved as well. He was the father of Mali and gave the world peace. After him the world has not seen a greater conqueror, for he was the seventh and last conqueror. He had made the capital of an empire out of his father's village, and Niani became the navel of the earth. In the most distant lands Niani was talked of and foreigners said, 'Travellers from Mali can tell lies with impunity', for Mali was a remote country for many peoples.

The griots, fine talkers that they were, used to boast of Niani and Mali saying: 'If you want salt, go to Niani, for Niani is the camping place of the Sahel[77] caravans. If you want gold, go to Niani, for Bouré, Bambougou and Wagadou work for Niani. If you want fine cloth, go to Niani, for the Mecca road passes by Niani. If you want fish, go to Niani, for it is there that the fishermen of Maouti and Djenné come to sell their catches. If you want meat, go to Niani, the country of the great hunters, and the land of the ox and the sheep. If you want to see an army, go to Niani, for it there that the united forces of Mali are to be found. If you want to see a great king, go to Niani, for it is there that the son of Sogolon lives, the man with two names.'

This is what the masters of the spoken word used to sing.

I must mention Kita among the great cities of the empire, the city of holy water which became the second capital of the Keitas. I shall mention vanished Tabon, the iron-gated city. I shall not forget Do, nor Kri, the motherland of Sogolon, the buffalo woman. I shall also cite Koukouba, Batamba and Kambasiga, towns of the sofas. I shall mention the town of Diaghan, Mema, the town of hospitality, and Wagadou, where the descendants of

Alexander the Great used to reign. How many heaped-up ruins, how many vanished cities! How many wildernesses peopled by the spirits of great kings! The silk-cotton trees and baobabs that you see in Mali are the only traces of extinct cities.

Eternal Mali

How many piled-up ruins, how much buried splendour! But all the deeds I have spoken of took place long ago and they all had Mali as their background. Kings have succeeded kings, but Mali has always remained the same.

Mali keeps its secrets jealously. There are things which the uninitiated will never know, for the griots, their depositaries, will never betray them. Maghan Sundiata, the last conqueror on earth, lies not far from Niani-Niani at Balandougou, the weir town.[78]

After him many kings and many Mansas reigned over Mali and other towns sprang up and disappeared. Hajji Mansa Moussa, of illustrious memory, beloved of God, built houses at Mecca for pilgrims coming from Mali, but the towns which he founded have all disappeared, Karanina, Bouroun-Kouna—nothing more remains of these towns. Other kings carried Mali far beyond Djata's frontiers, for example Mansa Samanka and Fadima Moussa, but none of them came near Djata.[79]

Maghan Sundiata was unique. In his own time no one equalled him and after him no one had the ambition to surpass him. He left his mark on Mali for all time and his taboos still guide men in their conduct.

Mali is eternal. To convince yourself of what I have said go to Mali. At Tigan you will find the forest dear to Sundiata. There you will see Fakoli Koroma's plastron. Go to Kirikoroni near Niassola and you will see a tree which commemorates Sundiata's passing through these parts. Go to Bankoumana on the Niger and you will see Soumaoro's balafon, the balafon which is called Balguintiri. Go to Ka-ba and you will see the clearing of Kouroukan Fougan, where the great assembly took place which gave Sundiata's empire its constitution. Go to Krina near Ka-ba and you will see the bird that foretold the end to Soumaoro. At Keyla, near Ka-ba, you will find the royal drums belonging to Djolo-fin Mansa, king of Senegal, whom Djata defeated. But never try, wretch, to pierce the mystery which Mali hides from you. Do not go and disturb the spirits in their eternal rest. Do not ever go into the dead cities to question the past, for the spirits never forgive. Do not seek to know what is not to be known.

*　　*　　*

Men of today, how small you are beside your ancestors, and small in mind too, for you have trouble in grasping the meaning of my words. Sundiata rests near Niani-Niani, but his spirit lives on and today the Keitas still come and bow before the stone under which lies the father of Mali.

To acquire my knowledge I have journeyed all round Mali. At Kita I saw the mountain where the lake of holy water sleeps; at Segou, I learnt the history of the kings of Do and Kri; at Fadama, in Hamana, I heard the Kondé griots relate how the Keitas, Kondés and Kamaras conquered Wouroula.[80] At Keyla, the village of the great masters, I learnt the origins of Mali and the art of speaking. Everywhere I was able to see and understand what my masters were teaching me, but between their hands I took an oath to teach only what is to be taught and to conceal what is to be kept concealed.

Notes

1. The twelve doors of Mali refer to the twelve provinces of which Mali was originally composed. After Sundiata's conquests the number of conquests increased considerably. Early Mali seems to have been a confederation of the chief Mandingo tribes: Keita, Kondé, Traoré, Kamara and Koroma. D.T.N.

2. According to tradition Sundiata's mother had a buffalo for a totem, namely the fabulous buffalo which, it is said, ravaged the land of Do. The lion is the totem and ancestor of the Keitas. Thus, through his father Sundiata is the son of the lion, and, through his mother, the son of the buffalo. D.T.N.

3. I have used this word 'Mandingo' to mean the people who inhabited Mali and their language, and as an adjective to mean anything pertaining to these people, though the adjective 'Mandingan' exists too. Old Mali, where much of the action of this story takes place, is a vaguely defined area between the Niger and Sankarani rivers and should not be confused with the modern Republic of Mali of which it is only a fraction. G.D.P.

   The inhabitants of Mali call themselves Maninka or Mandinka. Malli and Malinke are the Fulani deformations of the words Manding and Mandinka respectively. 'Mali' in the Mandingo language means 'a hippopotamus' and it is not impossible that Mali was the name given to one of the capitals of the emperors. One tradition tells us that Sundiata changed himself into a hippopotamus in the Sankarani river. So it is not astonishing to find villages in old Mali which have 'Mali' for a name. This name could have formerly been that of a city. In old Mali there is one village called Mali-koma, i.e. New Mali. D.T.N.

4. Bilali Bounama was the first muezzin and the Companion of the Prophet Muhammad. Like most medieval Muslim dynasties, the Mali emperors were careful to link themselves with the Prophet's family, or at least with someone near to him. In the fourteenth

85

century we will see Mansa Moussa return to Mali after his pilgrimage with some representatives of the Arab tribe of Qureish (Muhammad's tribe) in order to bring down the Prophet of God's blessing on his empire. After Kankan Moussa, several princes of Mali were to imitate him, notably Askia Muhammad in the sixteenth century. D.T.N.

This Askia Muhammad (1493–1528) ruled the Songhay Empire which overran that of Mali, but Muhammad's surname—Touré—indicates his Mandingo origin and in this sense he can be styled a 'prince of Mali'. G.D.P.

5. The Mandingo word is 'Simbon' and it literally means 'a hunter's whistle', but it is also used as an honorific title to denote a great hunter, a title which Sundiata later bore. The funeral wake which the hunters of a district organize in honour of a dead colleague is called 'Simbon-si'. D.T.N.

6. Kondolon Ni Sané is a dual hunting deity. Kondolon is a god of the chase and has Sané as an inseparable companion. These two deities are always linked and they are invoked as a pair. This dual deity has the property of being everywhere at once and when it reveals itself to the hunter the latter frequently comes across game. The guardianship of the bush and forest devolves on this deity and it is also the symbol of union and friendship. One must never invoke them separately at the risk of incurring very severe punishments. The two deities sometimes rival each other in skill but never fall out. In Hamana (Kouroussa) Mamadi Kani is accredited with the oath which the hunter takes before being received as a Simbon. Here is the oath:

(a) Will you resolve to satisfy Kondolon Ni Sané before your own father? (i.e. one should opt for the Master Hunter when confronted with an order from him and a conflicting order from one's own father.)

(b) Will you learn that respect does not mean slavery and give respect and submission at all times to your Master Hunter?

(c) Will you learn that cola is good, tobacco is good, honey is sweet, etc.—and give them over to your Master?

If the answer is 'yes' the apprentice hunter is accepted. In certain provinces of Siguiri, this oath is attributed to a certain Allah Mamadi who was not a king. D.T.N.

7. All the traditions acknowledge that the little village of Niani was the first capital of Mali and the residence of the first kings. It is said that Sundiata made it into a great city and thus it was called 'Niani-ba'—Niani the Great. Today it is a little village of a few hundred inhabitants on the Sankarani river and one kilometre from the frontier of the republics of Guinea and Mali. In the songs to Sundiata the town also bears the name of Niani-Niani, which is an emphatic title. D.T.N.

8. The silk-cotton tree of Malabar is the tree referred to here. It was brought to West Africa by the Portuguese in the fourteenth to fifteenth centuries so their frequent mention here is anachronistic, for the action described in this book took place between about 1217 and 1237. G.D.P.

9. The word M. Niane uses is 'Baraka' and it means blessing or the gift of divine power, to which our word 'grace' approximates. The word is fully discussed by Trimingham in his *Islam in West Africa*, pp. 111–12. G.D.P.

10. See note 5.

11. A hunter's bag is called 'sassa' in the original. It is a sort of goat-skin but there are several different kinds. Usually hunters have a little sassa for their personal fetishes. D.T.N.

12. The clear language *par excellence* is Mandingo. For the Mandingoes their language is clear like their country of open savannas, which they often contrast with the dark forest—hence references to Mali as the 'Bright Country'. D.T.N.

13. The land of Do seems to be the present-day region of Segou. Tradition speaks of Do as a powerful country. In modern times Do has been associated with the land of Kri and hence one speaks of 'Do ni Kri'. It is the land of ten thousand guns according to tradition and here is a poem which extols the land of Do:

> Land of ten cities
> Where Mansa Oumalé Kondé reigns,
> Do and Kri
> Land of the guns, Diarra
> Do and Kri.   D.T.N.

14. In Mali the great harvest takes place in November and December. The young men, freed after these great labours, leave the villages, perhaps to seek a little fortune, or perhaps for the mere love of travel. They generally return a little before the great rains in May and June. D.T.N.

15. Most West African tribes believe in wraiths or doubles, but beliefs vary and are often difficult to determine even for one tribe. The Mandingoes believe that there are two spiritual principles in man; the life principle (ni) which returns to God at death, and the wraith or double (dya) which can leave the body during sleep, and after death stays in the house of mourning until the performance of ritual sacrifices releases it to wander among the places frequented by the dead person until, after fifty years, it rejoins the ni. Much of the activity of the double in this book, however, seems better explained by references to the Hausa concepts of 'kurwa' and 'iska'. For a full discussion of all these ideas see Trimingham, op. cit., pp. 58–60. G.D.P.

16. According to tradition, it was at the death of the buffalo that the distinction between Traoré and Dioubaté arose. The two brothers Oulani and Oulamba were both Traorés. When the younger had killed the buffalo, Oulamba, the elder, composed off the cuff a song to the victor which said: 'Brother, if you were a griot, nobody would resist you,' in Mandingo: 'Koro toun Bake Djeli a Dian-Bagate.' The expression 'Dian-Baga-te' became 'Diabate' and by corruption 'Dioubaté'. Thus the Dioubaté griots are related to the Traorés. D.T.N.

17. From this ludicrous choice the Traorés and Kondés became 'sana-khou' which might be expressed by the coined word 'banter-brothers'. It means that as a token of some historical relationship two tribes or clans acquired the right to poke fun at one another with impunity. 'Banter-brotherhood' exists among many tribes of the savanna zone to this day. I once heard my servant allow himself to be called a bastard by a member of a tribe related to his only by this curious bond, and he merely laughed at this very grave insult. G.D.P.

18. The giving of cola nuts marks the opening of any sort of negotiation among the Mandingoes, and in this case the negotiation of a marriage. G.D.P.

19. The 'bolon' is a three-stringed instrument similar to the 'kora' which, however, has twenty-seven strings. The music of the bolon is war music whereas the kora is for domootio music. D.T.N.

20. A bloodstained cloth which showed publicly that the marriage had been consummated and that the bride had been a virgin. G.D.P.

21. Sand was used in divination and could give messages to the initiated. G.D.P.

22. The blood is the vehicle of the spiritual principles in man, of which the wraith is one. Shedding blood releases these principles, congealing paralyses them. G.D.P.

23. Owls are birds of ill-omen in West Africa, supposed to contain the spirits of the dead. G.D.P.

24. The 'tabala' was the royal ceremonial drum, one of the insignia of Muslim kingship. G.D.P.

25. The 'balafon' is an instrument like a xylophone made of blocks of wood set on gourds. G.D.P.

26. Maghan the Handsome. G.D.P.

27. Sundiata's gluttony was also legendary and some connect his surname with this: Soun (thief)—Djata (lion). It is said that he went marauding from house to house. According to another tradition (the one I have adopted), the name of Sundiata came from a contraction of his mother's name, Sogolon, placed before the name of the son, Djata, a very frequent practice among the Mandingoes. This gives Sogolon Djata—So-on Djata. The exact pronunciation in Mandingo lands is 'Sondjata'. D.T.N.

28. It is customary for West African boys to go for a few months to 'bush school' where they learn tribal lore in preparation for circumcision at the age of about twelve, when they become fully initiated members of the tribe. G.D.P.

29. I have been unable to find out the botanical name for this plant so I have used the word as it appears in the original. G.D.P.

30. The baobab is sometimes known as the monkey bread tree; its leaves are used for flavouring. G.D.P.

31. It was the custom to send princes of one court to be brought up in another. The political motive was twofold. The princes would probably preserve their boyhood friendships on coming to the throne, and while they were at the foreign court they could serve as hostages guaranteeing their fathers' loyalty. G.D.P.

32. M. Niane uses throughout the Mandingo name for Alexander, 'Djoulou Kara Naini', which is a corruption of the Arabic 'Dhu'l Qarnein'. G.D.P. In all the Mandingo traditions they like to compare Sundiata to Alexander. It is said that Alexander was the second last great conqueror of the world and Sundiata the seventh and last. D.T.N.

33. This oversight is in the original French. Sassouma Bérété offered the witches hay, not millet. G.D.P.

34. Wori is a very popular game in the western Sudan. It is like draughts, but the pieces are small stones laid out in holes bored in a tree-trunk. Millet, however, seems a more likely thing for her to offer. D.T.N.

35. Meetings and consultations were, and still are, held under a prominent tree. G.D.P.

36. Sundiata here addresses Mansa Konkon in the familiar second person singular. G.D.P.

37. The Mandingoes are part of a racial group including Bambaras, Sossos (pron. Soosoos) and Diallonkés, all speaking closely related languages and occupying adjacent territory; these we can refer to as tribes. Within these tribes there are clans such as the Traorés, Keitas, Kondés and Kamaras, who speak the same language but claim different ancestors and totems. Among these clans there are castes of craftsmen, endogamous groups with their own rituals, protective deities, etc. One of the most important castes was that of the smiths who, in an iron age society, had the power to make the best weapons and use them to their own advantage. After Islamization these castes held on to many of their pagan practices and became feared for their occult powers, though they occupied an inferior social position and kept to their own villages. Hence in this book smiths are often mentioned as being great sorcerers or soothsayers. G.D.P.

38. Wagadou is the Mandingo name for the land of old Ghana reigned over by the Tounkara-Cissé princes. D.T.N.

In translating I have made a distinction which does not appear in the original since M. Niane uses the word Wagadou throughout. I have used Wagadou to mean the city where the Cissé kings reigned and Ghana, a more familiar word to English readers, to mean the empire as a whole. In fact, in Sundiata's day Ghana had been reduced to the area of the city of Wagadou and its environs. G.D.P.

39. The distance was approximately 550 km. G.D.P.

40. I have used the word 'taboo' to translate the French *pacte*. M. Niane explains that the original word is 'dio', a prohibition pronounced by an ancestor and which the descendants must respect. Here the taboo relates to the well-known legend of the snake of Wagadou. This city had as a protective jinn a gigantic snake to which a young woman was sacrificed every year. The choice having fallen on the beautiful Sia, her betrothed, Mamadou Lamine (called 'Amadou the Silent' by other traditions), cut off the snake's head and saved his beloved. Ever after, calamities kept falling on the city, whose inhabitants fled following a drought which struck the whole country. It is in any case difficult to fix the date of the disappearance of Wagadou. According to Delafosse the city was annihilated by Sundiata himself in 1240, but Ibn Khaldun still mentions an interpreter from Ghana at the end of the fourteenth century. D.T.N.

41. The original gives 'serpent-Bida'. G.D.P.

42. The white traders referred to were probably Moors from the Sahara. G.D.P.

43. The Soninke are a tribe related to the Mandingoes but interpenetrated by Berbers and Fulanis. They were Islamized earlier than other West African tribes and thus gained the reputation of being very religious. They are also great traders and travellers. See Trimingham, op. cit., pp. 13–14. G.D.P.

44. The French word is *marabout*, but it is used in West Africa to mean a Muslim cleric or divine, or even someone who is merely very religious, as the distinction between clergy and laity is not marked. G.D.P.

45. Mandingo. G.D.P.

46. 'Sofas' are Sudanese infantrymen, or soldiers, warriors generally. D.T.N.

47. Diaghan lay on either side of the Falémé river, a tributary of the Senegal. The Diarisso dynasty was founded by a certain Kambine in the eleventh century and was formed from Soninke refugees who had escaped the attacks of the Almoravids by fleeing south from Ghana. Soumaoro (sometimes spelt Soumangourou) was the son of a Soninke warrior, Djara of the Kanté clan. Some scholars think that the present-day Sossos who inhabit the coastal region of Guinea had nothing to do with Soumaoro's city of Sosso. M. Niane, however, maintains that they are the descendants of Soumaoro's followers who fled to the Fouta Djallon after their leader's defeat at Krina. G.D.P.

48. The material symbol which is the abode of some supernatural power, e.g. a statuette, altar, mask, etc. See Trimingham, op. cit., p. 104. G.D.P.

49. Like many other African cities, Sosso seems to have been an agglomeration of villages belonging to distinct clans or castes. G.D.P.

50. The 'Vulture Tune', with the 'Hymn to the Bow', is frequently mentioned in the text. They are traditional songs still current among the Mandingoes. D.T.N.

51. Here is one of the dicta that often recurs in the mouths of the traditional griots. This explains the parsimony with which these vessels of historical traditions give their knowledge away. According to them, the Whites have vulgarized knowledge. When a White knows something everybody knows it. One would have to be able to change this state of mind if one wanted to know some day all that the griots decline to give away. D.T.N.

52. The mithkal was an Arab measurement of weight equal to 4·25 grammes. In Mandingo this term is used to denote the smallest fraction of something. D.T.N.

53. Some traditions say that Fakoli's wife, Keleya, managed on her own to regale the whole army with her cooking, while the three hundred wives of Soumaoro never managed to feed the troops to their satisfaction. Jealous, Soumaoro abducted Keleya. This

was the origin of Fakoli's defection. He rallied to Sundiata. D.T.N.

54. It is known that in the forest region of Guinea, south of Kankan, many Mansaré/Keitas are to be found. It is said that they are the descendants of Dankaran Touman, who colonized (Mandingized) the whole region of Kissidougou. These Keitas are called Farmaya Keita. It is said that when Dankaran Touman arrived on the site of Kissidougou he cried, 'An bara kissi' (We are saved), whence the name given to the town. Kissidougou is thus, etymologically, the city of safety. D.T.N.

A bit dubious, I feel. The dominant tribe in that area is the Kissi tribe and 'dougou' is a common ending for place names in this region. G.D.P.

55. I have been unable to find the botanical name for this so I use the original. G.D.P.

56. Mother. G.D.P.

57. Bouré is the region to the north-west of Siguiri in Guinea. G.D.P.

58. 'Daffeké' is an emphatic word for 'a fine charger'. D.T.N.

59. The tradition of Dioma represents the battle of Kankigne as a semi-defeat for Sundiata:

> Kankigne Tabe bara djougouya
> Djan ya bara bogna mayadi.

'The battle of Kankigne was terrible; men were less dignified than slaves there.' D.T.N.

60. The word I have translated as 'pennant' is 'bandari' which comes from the Arabic and means a banner, standard, flag, pennant. Another word also borrowed from Arabic is 'raya' which denotes a banner formerly carried by great clerics on the move. Even now regional chiefs still raise their 'bandari' above their house. D.T.N.

61. 'N'Ko' means 'I say' in Mandingo. The Mandingoes like to distinguish themselves from other peoples by their language. For them, Mandingo is the 'Kan gbe' (clear language *par excellence*). All those who say 'N'Ko' are, in theory, Mandingoes. D.T.N.

62. A 'tana' is a hereditary taboo, and can also mean a totem, i.e. the object of the taboo. In this case Soumaoro was forbidden to touch

ergot, of which a cock's spur is composed, and as long as he observed this he could concentrate in himself the power of his ancestors. On his touching ergot and thus breaking the taboo his ancestors withdrew their power and his downfall followed. Power and life-force are regarded as communal possessions in Africa and when a man cuts himself off from the group by breaking a taboo he is as good as dead unless he performs a sacrifice in expiation. G.D.P.

63. This is an expression of joy in Mandingo. D.T.N.

64. 'Fama-Djan' means 'the tall chief'. Later, particularly under Kankan Moussa, 'Fama' was to be the title of provincial governors, the word 'Farin' being reserved for military governors. 'Ke-Farin' means 'valorous warrior'. D.T.N.

65. Forward. D.T.N.

66. There are numerous versions of Soumaoro's end. Here it is the Hamana version. That of Dioma says that Soumaoro, pursued by Sundiata, invoked his protective jinn for the last time, asking them not to let him fall into Sundiata's hands. So he was transformed into stone on the mountain of Koulikoro. Other traditions say that Soumaoro, hit by the cock's spur at Krina, disappeared right on the battlefield. The fact remains that after Krina the king of Sosso is never heard of again. His son Balla, captured by Fakoli, was taken in captivity to Mali. D.T.N.

67. The bourein is a dwarf shrub which grows in poor ground. It is a savanna variety of gardenia. Its use in the kitchen is forbidden and it is a shrub of ill-omen. D.T.N.

68. Diaghan was the town of Dia, which, according to the traditions, was a town of great divines. The Diawara reigned at Dia; the name means 'Wild Beast of Dia'. D.T.N.

69. The Keitas. G.D.P.

70. On the emperor's stay at Kita it is the Dioma version that I have followed. The Keitas of Dioma claim that their ancestor, a grandson of Sundiata, left Kita to come and settle in Dioma. Kiat was one of the big towns of the empire. D.T.N.

71. It is generally believed that Ka-ba (the present-day Kangaba) was one of the earliest residences of the Keitas. Local tradition states

that the Keitas did not settle there until after Sundiata. Kangaba is a foundation of the Sibi Kamaras and the Traorés. The Keitas who settled there came from Mali in this way. There were two brothers of whom the younger, Bemba Kanda, left his brother at the halting-place of Figuera-Koro, came and settled at Ka-ba and allied himself to the Kamaras. In consequence several Keita families came and settled there. D.T.N.

72. The dynasty Sundiata founded is always treated as a Muslim dynasty though outside of the royal tribe Islam was weak and, as the text shows, mixed with a lot of pagan survivals. G.D.P.

73. King of kings. D.T.N.

74. 'Mansa' is a title equivalent to emperor or paramount king. The French version often has 'roi' before Mansa as if Mansa were a name. I have followed this in translating, but it is not strictly correct. G.D.P.

75. This song is one of the most famous which Balla Fasséké composed to Sundiata. It expresses the idea that Sogolon's son was the rampart behind which everyone found refuge. In other songs also attributed to Balla Fasséké Sundiata is constantly compared to Alexander (cf. recording number L.D.M. 30.081 'Vogue' made by Keita Fodeba). For my part I am inclined to attribute these songs to griots of the time of Kankan Moussa (1307–1332). In fact at that time the griots knew general history much better, at least through Arabic writings and especially the Koran. D.T.N.

76. The original has 'moude', a Mandingo deformation of Arabic 'mudd', which is a cereal measure, in fact, the legal measure fixed by the Prophet. As the taxes were paid in kind they were calculated by the mudd and finally the word came to mean simply a tax. A mudd of rice weighed 10–15 kilos, i.e. the contents of a basket of rice. D.T.N.

77. The Sahel is the region of the Sudan bordering on the Sahara. G.D.P.

78. Here Djeli Mamadou Kouyaté declined to go any further. However, there are many accounts of Sundiata's end. The first says that Sundiata was killed by an arrow in the course of public demonstration in Niani. The second, very popular in Mali, is rendered

feasible by the presence of Sundiata's tomb near the Sankarani. According to the second account Sundiata was drowned in the Sankarani and was buried near the very place where he was drowned. I have heard this version from the mouths of several traditionists, but following what events did Sundiata meet his death in the waters? That is the question to which a reply must be found. D.T.N.

79. Here Djeli Mamadou Kouyaté mentions several kings of Mali. Hajji Mansa Moussa is no other than the famous Kankan Moussa (1307–1332) made for ever illustrious by his celebrated pilgrimage in 1325. The Dioma tradition attributes to Kankan Moussa the foundation of many towns which have now disappeared. D.T.N.

80. Griot traditionists travel a great deal before being 'Belen-Tigui'— Master of Speech in Mandingo. This expression is formed from 'belen', which is the name for the tree-trunk planted in the middle of the public square and on which the orator rests when he is addressing the crowd. 'Tigui' means 'master of'. There are several famous centres for the study of history, e.g. Fadama in Hamana (Kouroussa), situated on the right bank of the Niandan opposite Baro; but more especially Keyla, the town of traditionists; and Diabaté near Kangaba (Ka-ba), Republic of Mali. Mamadou Kouyaté is from the village of Djeliba Koro in Dioma (south of Siguiri), a province inhabited by the Keitas who came from Kita at the end of the fourteenth century and the beginning of the fifteenth century (see my *Diplôme d'Etudes Superieures*). D.T.N.

Also in Longman African Classics

Fools and other stories

Njabulo Ndebele

Winner of the Noma Award 1983

'And when victims spit upon victims should they not be called fools?
Fools of darkness.'

A taut, lyrical and compelling collection of stories, vividly bringing
to life the black urban locations of apartheid South Africa.

These are rich and enchanting stories told with the warmth of
childhood memory: of the adulation of a child for his trumpet-
playing uncle; a teenager's trial of endurance to prove himself
worthy of his street-gang; a child's rebellion against his parents
snobbish aspirations.

And the title story, *Fools*, tells with painful intensity of events sparked
by a meeting between a disgraced teacher, haunted by the impotence
of his present life, and a student activitist railing against those who
do not share his sense of urgency.

The author believes 'we have given away too much of our real and
imaginative lives to the opressor'. These beautiful award-winning
stories of township life in all its complexity are his answer.

'Njabulo Ndebele's first book represents the kind of beginning in
fiction that will prove to have altered the contours of our literature
... His storytelling is full-fleshed and elegant ... of thrilling
significance'.

Lionel Abrahams *Sesame*

'Brings with it an exhilerating current of fresh air ... solid, vibrant
prose'.

E'skia Mphahlele *The Sowetan*

ISBN 0 582 78621 5

Hungry Flames and other Black South African Short Stories

Edited by Mbulelo Mzamane

From the bare concrete of the crowded prisons to the carpeted drawing rooms of the new African middle class, these fifteen short stories by South Africa's finest Black writers paint an urgent and vital picture of contemporary South Africa.

These stories rank with those of Steinbeck and Hemingway in their honest portraits of working men and women in all their strengths and in all their weaknesses — all of them living in the shadow of the apartheid state.

Ove fifty years of Black South African writing in English is represented in this collection. A critical introduction describes the evolution of writing from the pioneers, such as R.R.R. Dhlomo and Sol Plaatje, through the urban 'jazz' style of the fifties to the more politicised Black Consciousness writers of the Sharpeville and Soweto eras.

The editor, Mbulelo Mzamane, is himself a distinguished writer of short stories and is the author of *My Cousin Comes to Jo'burg* (1982) and of *The Children of Soweto* (1982). He now teaches in the Department of English, Ahmadu Bello University, Zaria in Nigeria.

ISBN 0 582 78590 1

The Last Duty

Isidore Okpewho

Winner of the African Arts Prize for Literature

Against the backcloth of a violent and murderous civil war six individuals linked by conflicting ties of honour, greed, lust, fear and love play out a drama of their own that is no less bloody than the war itself. The resolution of the drama has the cathartic force of classical tragedy as the individuals recognise their final duty to reclaim their self-respect from the quagmire of corruption and betrayal into which they have all been led.

'*The Last Duty* is a highly sophisticated and successfully achieved piece of work . . . an imaginative reconstruction of the experience of the Nigerian Civil War. In its deep moral concern and in its technical accomplishment, *The Last Duty* has earned an honourable place in the development of African literature'.

British Book News

'C'est un beau livre' *Afrique Contemporaine*

'A strong and original voice in Nigerian literature' *Books Abroad*

ISBN 0 582 78535 9

Scarlet Song

Mariama Ba

Translated by Dorothy S. Blair

Mariama Ba's first novel So Long a Letter was the winner of the Noma Award in 1980. In this her second and, tragically, last novel she displays all the same virtues of warmth and crusading zeal for women's rights that won her so many admirers for her earlier work.

Mireille, daughter of a French diplomat and Ousmane, son of a poor Muslim family in Senegal, are two childhood sweethearts forced to share their love in secret. Their marriage shocks and dismays both sets of parents, but it soon becomes clear that their youthful optimism and love offer a poor defence against the pressures of society. As Ousmane is lured back to his roots, Mireille is left humiliated, isolated and alone.

The tyranny of tradition and chauvinism is brilliantly exposed in this passionate plea for human understanding. The author's sympathetic insights into the condition of women deserve recognition throughout the world.

ISBN 0 582 78595 2

Tales of Amadou Koumba

Birago Diop

Translated by Dorothy S. Blair

Retold with wit and charm, this classic collection of folk tales by the 'poet of the African bush' stands comparison with the fables of Aesop and La Fontaine. Originally told to Diop by his family's *griot*, these tales take us back and forth between the surreal world of the miraculous and the profound reality of African daily life.

'The poetic nature of Birgao Diop's writing, in its primitive majesty, is in direct line from the Griots and the oral tradition'.

Jean-Paul Sartre

'Everything in this subtle and perceptive work is a delight'.

Présence Africaine

'This show of African wisdom, constitutes, without a shadow of doubt, the finest prose work in our African literature'.

Afrique en Marche

ISBN 0 582 78587 1